MAKE YOUR BUSINESS OUR BUSINESS

NEW AND UPDATED INCLUDING
2020-2021-GUIDELINES AND REMOTE NOTARIZATION

AN INTERACTIVE, STEP-BY-STEP GUIDE TO

POLICIES, PROCEDURES & PROFITS

AVOID THE PITFALLS OF STARTING A NEW BUSINESS

CALL EXPERTS DANIEL AND JUDITH AND ASK ABOUT COACHING SERVICES

CHECK OUT MAKEYOURBUSINESSOURBUSINESS.COM FOR FORMS, SUPPLIES AND REFERENCES

By **DANIEL C. LEWIS** and **JUDITH P. LAWRENCE**

Print ISBN: 978-1-09837-276-7

eBook ISBN: 978-1-09837-277-4

DEDICATION FROM JUDI LAWRENCE

To four wonderful women who each contributed to my being the woman I am;

My Mom, Aunt Bev, Aunt Mick and Aunt Ruth.

And to my Uncle Chuck, who led by example, teaching me that if you work hard, you can accomplish anything.

I miss them.

DEDICATION FROM DANIEL LEWIS

This book is dedicated to all those notaries and business people who have inspired me to write this book but will never read it.

SO, YOU HAVE AN IDEA!

Your work is going to fill a large part of your life, and the only way to be truly satisfied is to do what you believe is great work. And the only way to do great work is to love what you do. If you haven't found it yet, keep looking. Don't settle. As with all matters of the heart, you'll know when you find it."

—Steve Jobs

- A six-foot purple dinosaur named Barney stars in the children's TV show **Barney** and Friends. The character got his start in 1987 in direct-sale videos created by Dallas teacher Sheryl Leach. The tapes caught the eye of the Public Broadcasting System, who put Barney and Friends on the air in 1992.

- Xavier Roberts, a 21-year-old art student, used quilting skills he learned from his mother to develop a line of hand-stitched, one-of-a-kind, soft fabric sculptures he called "The Little People," found in a magical cabbage patch. They were not offered for sale but were "adopted," each with his or her own individual name and birth certificate. **Cabbage Patch Kids** are now one of the longest-running doll franchises in the country.

- **YouTube** is an American video-sharing website headquartered in San Bruno, California. The service was created by three former PayPal employees-Chad Hurley, Steve Chen, and Jawed Karim—in February 2005. Google bought the site in November 2006 for $1.65 billion; YouTube now operates as one of Google's subsidiaries.

Most businesses begin with an idea – it is what you do with that idea that makes the difference.

I was at a crossroads in my own life and didn't know what to do. I was selling my home and needed a notary, which I paid for. That was a light bulb for me and that is how my first company was born. Starting a notary company was easy for me because I was in familiar territory. Moving into mortgages and refinances was comfortable because I had worked for attorneys all my adult life and I had familiarity with such documents.

Daniel Lewis and Judith Lawrence will teach you our PPP theory—

Policies, Procedures, and **Profits**.

Talk to your family and friends. You have the Internet to help you. There are sites that will listen to your ideas and offer you their assistance.

A MESSAGE TO OUR READERS:

You are about to read how to create your new business. We want you to know that many of the topics you will read about tell you to seek advice from experts, including an accountant, a technology expert, and a webmaster, to name a few. These people will become important to you as you take this journey, but it is important to remember that this is **YOUR BUSINESS** and **YOU** make the final decisions.

When you decide on who you are going to work with, it is important that you choose people who "get you" and who you feel comfortable talking to. You will need to show your accountant how much money you are spending, and you will need to tell your website designer that you just don't like the new design he or she slaved over. Take your time, interview these people and try to make the best decisions you can. And should you make a wrong decision, as we all do, cut your losses and move on as soon as you know.

It should be an exciting time. Especially in the beginning, you will feel overwhelmed by the decisions that need to be made. Keep a notebook; jot down what people tell you. Later, that will become an invaluable resource.

At **MAKE YOUR BUSINESS OUR BUSINESS**, our advice to you is to listen carefully, do your own research, and make not only well-informed decisions but decisions you feel will be congruent with the vision you see for your business.

We are available to answer questions and consult with you every step along the way.

Contact Daniel and Judith at MakeYourBusinessOurBusiness@gmail.com

What are you going to do with your life today?

FORWARD

"When written in Chinese, the word 'crisis' is composed of two characters. One represents danger and the other represents opportunity."

-John F. Kennedy

The authors decided to update this book because in the early part of2020 life for notary entrepreneurs changed drastically. Not since the Swine influenza back in 1918 has the world encountered a pandemic of this magnitude. Notaries have had to acclimate themselves to what is called the "new normal". Curbside closings, Remote Notarizations are just some of the new normal for4 notaries. Other changes include:

Notaries have had to improvise as to setting up signing assignments in signer(s') homes (signing in garages, back patios as opposed to the home of the signer(s);

Notaries not being able to go into hospitals, nursing homes, or assisted living facilities but instead signing through a window;

Notaries experiencing several Secretaries of States Offices operating with reduced staff creating delays in approval on basic transactions such as Apostilles.

After March 2020 notary entrepreneurs all over the country experienced massive changes to their businesses. Both authors of this book wanted to revise this book to help you, the readers, navigate through these challenging times and thrive as a notary entrepreneur. We wanted to give you the most up-to-date information for your notary business library. Using this book as a tool for your notary business should increase your chances for success while decreasing your risk of failure.

Use this book to EXCEL.

WHY YOU SHOULD
READ THIS BOOK

You don't want to just add this book to your bookshelf. You want to read it often and apply it instantly.

The wisdom and experience shared by the authors of **MAKE YOUR BUSINESS OUR BUSINESS** will give you clarity and will entice you to read it again and again. So many books in this industry promise solutions that will get you the results you want. This book **actually delivers**. It will provide the tools to help you think bigger with more positive changes in your work life. Using this book properly will have an enormous impact on your business.

The profession of the notary public has changed over the years. It has evolved from being notary public employees working in a bank or insurance companies to becoming independent contractors, proctors for exams, insurance inspectors, and notary signing agents. This industry has over 4.5 million notary publics, with only a fraction of them knowing the true power and value of the office. This book is your gateway to a new adventure. It has been written by two successful notary publics in two different areas of the country. One of the authors has over 30 years of legal experience and now is a successful business owner. The other author has the perspective of running a very successful signing agent and rescheduling company. Both authors will give you a valuable and different perspectives on this industry.

This book will give you large ideas and tools to get you out of your own way and achieve success. Reading the book will give you step-by-step instructions on how to be successful.

HOW TO USE THIS BOOK

This book is meant to be a manual for people that want to be an entrepreneur and specifically a notary entrepreneur. Whether you are just starting your notary business, or you are a very seasoned Notary Signing Agent, this book is for you. To get the full benefit of this book read it repeatedly.

The content in this book will make you stop and think about how you could operate your business better. At **MAKE YOUR BUSINESS OUR BUSINESS**, our motto is *learning the policies*, *adhere to the procedures* and you will see immediate *profitability*.

That is the intent of this book. In some areas of this book, you will see parts that have "Warning Signs" such as the one below. These are signals to express the importance of the content. Please be sure you pay special attention to these Warning Signs.

You also want to look at the "Did You Know" section. Here we have snippets of interesting opportunities for notaries which you may want to consider taking advantage of.

At the beginning of the book we have inserted links to every Secretary of State for your easy convenience, so you can check your own state guidelines. We have also inserted links to some interesting articles and some great quotes from business people.

We guarantee that using this book daily will increase your efficiency and effectiveness.

THE ALTERNATIVE TO NOT READING THIS BOOK MIGHT RESULT IN YOUR SETTING UP AND/OR RUNNING YOUR NEW BUSINESS WITHOUT LEARNING ABOUT POLICIES, PROCEDURES, AND PROFITS.

I . GENERAL BUSINESS

FINANCIAL PLANNING FOR THE NOTARY ENTREPRENEUR

A notary entrepreneur is a business owner who has developed a successful business plan around helping his or her community as a notary public. Notary entrepreneurs are the drivers of innovation in their field. They organize, manage and assume all the risks of their notary business enterprise. If you have considered becoming a notary entrepreneur, here are four financial reasons that might just sway your thinking.

TAX ADVANTAGES

Without a doubt, there are several tax advantages to being a notary entrepreneur. Being a notary entrepreneur means keeping track of these different types of expenditures. Even though you don't have an employer matching your savings, you are able to put aside a lot of money in tax-deferred accounts and can choose a retirement plan that works best for you. Some of the most common tax deductions for business owners are meals, entertainment, travel, transportation, home office, internet, phone, health, and business insurance. To gain a better understanding of each tax deduction, see a tax professional.

OPPORTUNITY FOR INCREASED RETIREMENT SAVINGS

Being a notary entrepreneur allows you many options and incentives as far as financial planning. Since self-employed individuals must fund their retirement completely on their own, the contribution limits are far more generous than the limits placed if you were working as an employee.

We recommend you seek out a financial professional and receive as much advice about securing your financial future. There are many tax-deferred programs as well as other programs that will help you grow your investment in your future rapidly. As a self-employed person, you can prioritize your retirement planning and create a nice healthy nest egg.

Programs like a SIMPLE IRA, a Simplified Employee Pension (SEP) IRA and a Solo 401(k) can really help you to hit your financial goals.

For information about setting up a retirement savings program for yourself, email us at MakeYourBusinessOurBusiness@gmail.com.

UNLIMITED INCOME POTENTIAL

One of the greatest rewards of being a notary entrepreneur, as with any business owner, is that it gives you the opportunity to make an unlimited amount of income. Your income grows as your ability to be creative as a business owner grows. You have direct and complete control of how much income you ultimately make. Remember the greatest asset your business has is you.

It is definitely possible over the years to have earned millions of dollars from a typical 9 to 5 job. Operating at this level means you are competing against a number of people that want to achieve this same level of income. As a result, in today's job market your employer company may either get bought out, go out of business, or downsize before you get an opportunity to achieve your financial goals.

When you are a business owner and/or notary entrepreneur you can earn as much money as your talents, ambition, and energy levels will allow. Your income depends on your growth as a business professional.

BETTER CAREER SECURITY THAN A JOB

In the early 1990s, I began working for AT&T in middle management. I remember the first day after being hired, the training manager came into the room and said this will be the last job you will ever have. Two years later that same training manager was laid off in a companywide management layoff. Needless to say, job security is a thing of the past.

When you run your own business, no matter what it is, you may never face unemployment again. There will be times when your revenue may come in a bit slow; however, you will control who you do business with and for how long.

(Updated Action Steps) Write down the answers to each question:

1. What are your 3-5 year goals for your business?
2. How are you planning on tracking your business expenses each month?
3. What is your monthly retirement saving strategy?
4. What resources are you using to help you hit monthly financial goals?

For more information including webinars contact https://lewistraining.online/product/transitional-coaching-for-the-notary-entrepreneurs/

HOW TO WRITE
YOUR BUSINESS PLAN

A business plan is a written document that outlines what your business is, where it is going, and how it will get there. The business plan specifically outlines the financial objectives of your business and how it will position itself to achieve those goals.

In addition, a business plan is an indispensable tool to attract business capital.

Here are few tips for writing your business plan:

- Keep it short. Business plans should be clear and concise
- Talk about long-range goals and short-range goals
- Know your target audience
- Don't be intimidated; you have an idea, so sell it
- Discuss the problems and solutions
- Know Your competition
- Discuss positioning
- Discuss pricing
- Discuss timing – how long you think it will it take to accomplish your goals

The US Small Business Association offers courses on how to accomplish the writing of your plan: https://www.sba.gov/tools/sba-learning-center/training/how-write-business-plan

See also: How to Write a Business Plan for A Small Business https://www.wikihow.com/Write-a-Business-Plan-for-a-Small-Business

Use a Free Business Plan Builder: https://planbuildr.com/business-plan/new

To get help with writing your business plan, see: www.score.org

HOW T O WRITE Y OUR MISSION STATEMENT

A mission statement is a written declaration of your company's core purpose and focus. Your mission statement should clearly state which markets will be served and how you should communicate your intended direction for the company.

A mission statement is different from a vision in that the mission statement is more factual, a vision is a way you think things will be pursued to accomplish your goals.

In my opinion, although you will clearly have a **vision** for your company from the beginning, you might not want to write a mission statement until you are operational for a little while. Things change, your goals change, and opportunities present themselves that cause you to reevaluate the direction of your company.

https://articles.bplans.com/writing-a-mission-statement/

STARTING A NEW BUSINESS

WHETHER YOU ARE ALREADY AN ENTREPRENEUR, OR YOU ARE SEEKING TO BECOME AN ENTREPRENEUR, THE NEXT SEVERAL CHAPTERS WILL PROVIDE YOU WITH INFORMATION ON STARTING YOUR NEW BUSINESS

LOCAL GOVERNING BODIES OF EACH STATE FOR NOTARY PUBLICS

We are placing these websites at the beginning of this book for your convenience. Many times throughout the book we will suggest that you check your local state guidelines to ascertain specific state rules and regulations. Because our readers will be located throughout the United States, we thought this would make it easier for you to reference a link to the respective Secretary of State's offices. You will also find this useful in determining what each state requires for becoming a notary, insurance, etc. You can click on the link or copy the link and paste it in your browser.

Alabama	http://sos.alabama.gov/
Alaska	http://ltgov.alaska.gov/treadwell/notaries.html
American Samoa	http://americansamoa.gov/
Arizona	https://azsos.gov/business/notary-public
Arkansas	https://www.sos.arkansas.gov/ business-commercial- services-bcs/ notary-public-and-enotary
California	www.ss.ca.gov/business/notary/
Colorado	https://www.sos.state.co.us/pubs/notary/home.html
Connecticut	https://portal.ct.gov/SOTS/Business-Services/BSD
Delaware	http://notary.delaware.gov/

District of Columbia	https://os.dc.gov/service/ notary-and-authentication-services
Florida	http://notaries.dos.state.fl.us/index.html
Georgia	www.gsccca.org/projects/aboutnp.asp
Guam	www.guamattorneygeneral.com
Hawaii	http://hawaii.gov/ag/notary
Idaho	https://sos.idaho.gov/notaries- apostilles authentications/
Illinois	www.cyberdriveillinois.com/departments/index/ notary/home.html
Indiana	www.in.gov/sos/business/2378.htm
Iowa	https://sos.iowa.gov/notaries/about.html
Kansas	https://sos.ks.gov/business/notary.html
Kentucky	https://web.sos.ky.gov/notaries/Index
Louisiana	https://www.sos.la.gov/NotaryAndCertifications/ Pages/default.aspx
Maine	www.maine.gov/sos/cec/notary/notaries.html
Maryland	www.sos.state.md.us/notary/notary.aspx
Massachusetts	www.sec.state.ma.us/pre/prenot/notidx.htm
Michigan	www.michigan.gov/sos
Minnesota	https://www.sos.state.mn.us/notary-apostille/ become- a-notary/
Mississippi	https://www.sos.ms.gov/BusinessServices/Pages/ Notaries-Apostilles.aspx

Missouri	https://s1.sos.mo.gov/Business/Notary/newNotary
Montana	https://sosmt.gov/notary/applying-for-a-commission-new- and-renewal/
Nebraska	www.sos.state.ne.us/business/notary/
New Hampshire	https://sos.nh.gov/administration/administration/notary-public/
Nevada	https://sos.nh.gov/administration/administration/notary-public/
New Jersey	https://www.njportal.com/DOR/Notary
New Mexico	https://www.sos.state.nm.us/notary-and-apostille/
New York	www.dos.state.ny.us/licensing/
North Carolina	www.secretary.state.nc.us/notary North Dakotawww.nd.gov/sos/notaryserv
Northern Marianas	www.cnmigov.mp/government.php
Ohio	www.sos.state.oh.us/sos/recordsindexes/notary. aspx
Oklahoma	www.sos.state.ok.us/notary/notary_welcome.htm
Oregon	www.filinginoregon.com/notary/index.htm
Pennsylvania	www.dos.state.pa.us/notaries
Puerto Rico	www.ramajudicial,pr/odin/index.htm
Rhode Island	https://www.sos.ri.gov/divisions/notary-public/become-a- notary
South Carolina	https://sos.sc.gov/services-and-filings/notaries
South Dakota	https://sdsos.gov/

Tennessee	www.state.tn.us/sos/bus_svc/notary.htm
Texas	www.sos.state.tx.us/statdoc//index.shtml
Utah	http://notary.utah.g
Vermont	https://sos.vermont.gov/notaries-public/forms-instructions/
Virginia	https://www.commonwealth.virginia.gov/official-documents/notary-commissions/notary-application-process/
US Virgin Islands	https://ltg.gov.vi/departments/notary-public/
Washington	www.dol.wa.gov/business/notary
West Virginia	https://sos.wv.gov/business/Pages/NotaryFormsFees.aspx
Wisconsin	www.wdfi.org
Wyoming	http://soswy.state.wy.us/adminservices/notariesoverview.aspx

SHOULD **YOU** START A BUSINESS?

"My experience has been that work is almost the best way to pull oneself out of the depths."

—Eleanor Roosevelt

"The biggest risk is not taking any risk... In a world that's changing quickly, the only strategy that is guaranteed to fail is not taking risks."

—Mark Zuckerberg

The truth and nothing but the truth; becoming an entrepreneur is the most rewarding, most profitable, most exciting, and hardest thing you will ever do. Starting a business takes a 200% commitment. I am fond of telling people I get to work 7 days a week, I get to do the work, the bookkeeping, I get to make sure the office is neat and clean, and I get to worry about paying the bills. But I wake up every day with a sense of excitement as to what the day will bring.

Have a long talk with yourself and ask yourself if this is what you want? Ask yourself if you are willing to take a risk: Are you willing to give it whatever it takes, be it money, time, or sleep? And finally, ask yourself if you want to take the most exciting journey of your life?

Talk to your friends and family. If you have a spouse, a significant other or a partner, you need to have his or her support because, especially in the first year, this will require a serious amount of time. My friends continue to marvel (and sometimes make fun of) the serious commitment of time I make. My response is: if I were a surgeon and I had to operate on an emergency on a Sunday afternoon, no one would question it at all.

Here are a few articles I think you will enjoy:

The True Meaning of Entrepreneur
https://www.entrepreneur.com/article/244565

Entrepreneur Quiz – Should You Start a Business?
https://www.wesst.org/business-resources/entrepreneur-quiz/

BE PREPARED FOR
SOME HARD WORK

"When you play, play hard; when you work, don't play at all."

-Theodore Roosevelt

"The big secret in life is that there is no big secret. Whatever your goal, you can get there if you're willing to work."

-Oprah Winfrey

In the beginning, it is 12-hour days, 7 days a week.

People say to me all the time, "You work for yourself, you can do anything you want." Being a business owner, although my greatest accomplishment, is also the hardest I have ever worked. The success or failure of the business is in your hands. **THE BUCK STOPS WITH YOU.** You can only do anything you want when the client work is finished, all deadlines have been met, all calls have been returned, deposits have been made, invoicing has been done, and bills have been paid.

It's true, you get to be your own boss and in theory, that is kind of cool. But it is also true that when opportunity knocks on your door, you may have to give up some time with friends and/or family, or a date with Mr. or Mrs. Wonderful, to take advantage of that opportunity. In reality, for that period of time, the new client is the boss and if you want to get his or her work done and get paid for it, you have to do it. Someone once told me to remember, and sometimes to use it as part of a pitch, that you don't just want this job, but you want all future jobs this person may have to give you. People also tell me how lucky I am to be able to make my own hours. I often smile about that at the end of a busy and exhausting Sunday.

Want to hear the story of the 4:00 A.M. signing?

First, let me say this opportunity happened when I was in the notary business for about 2 months. I had ABSOLUTELY NO IDEA how much money I could charge for this service. I would not admit what I charged but it was one-fourth of what I should have.

I got the call about 7:00 P.M. The job was for a corporate executive (who called me himself, the first clue of how much he needed my services) who needed to get notary service on a document which was not scheduled to be ready for him to look at until 3:00 A.M., and which needed to be sent to a judge before 6:00 A.M.

> LESSON: HE NEEDED ME AT 4:00 A.M. HE HAD FEW OPTIONS. AS LONG AS I KEPT MY FEE REASONABLE, HE WOULD HAVE PAID WHAT HE HAD TO DO IN ORDER TO GET IT DONE.

To lower the risk of danger to myself, I took the following steps:

- I verified his credentials
- I found sufficient information, including his senior position with the company
- I located a photo; and
- I called a friend and told her who I would be working for and where I would be.

I took an Uber and arrived at 3:30 A.M., took care of the notarization and was back home by 4:15 A.M. The client and I shared an Uber home and the man could not thank me enough for my professionalism, and for just being there. He predicted that I was going to be successful in my business. I did not make a whole lot of money, but I gained a whole lot of confidence in myself and I made a friend who I continue to use as a reference.

Being self-employed, you do not receive a steady paycheck. When you are employed, if there is a major storm, you will still receive your check. If you are ill, hopefully, you have sick days to collect. If you are self-employed and no customers come calling, that is a financial setback. But on the other hand, if a client needs assistance at 4:00 A.M., and is willing to compensate you adequately, then you are ahead of the game.

Wow, so much negativity. Why would I want to do this?

Because that is part of the beginning, and I, being the eternal optimist, believed that in time, my business would be running well, and I would be able to take a little time and have lunch with a friend or go to a happy hour.

In the beginning, clients don't know you and have no loyalty to you. If you are not available, they usually just call the next notary shown on Google. But after a while, they know you, they know how hard you work and how available you are, and they are loyal to you. This year, for the first time, I took a quick trip to London with a friend. I was stunned when I got back to how many people left messages and said, "It's about time you took a few days off," or "I heard you are back on Tuesday; I'll be by with some documents."

Something else worth mentioning: in the beginning, I had no backup. Now I have a wonderful notary who, when I went to London, cared for my business. I was able to leave a message on my phone that if someone needed auto tags, call so and so, and if someone needed help on Sunday, call so and so. It is essential that you assemble a team of people who will act as your backup if needed.

SHOULD YOU HAVE
A HOME - BASED BUSINESS, OR
MUST YOU HAVE AN OFFICE?

I have been asked this question more times than I can count, and there is no definitive answer.

Much depends on what else is going on at home, the amount of space you need, the amount of space you have, and whether you are a structured person who can work at home without being distracted by television, telephone, children, etc.

I know many people who have successful businesses who work at home. Let's face it, it's less expensive, and if you like to work long hours, it is often easier not to have to bother to commute. I have one friend who outfitted her living room with several desks and has several people coming to work there every day. A home office can be perfect for a mobile signer who spends 80% of his or her time on the road and the other 20% with invoicing and other paperwork.

I had a different situation. I created my first company in my bedroom. I had a computer and a laser printer, a cabinet for supplies, and it began. And although I now have an office and a different name, that little company still gets calls every day.

I happened to stumble into a small, walk-in notary business that had been in the same location for over 30 years. It is probably one of a kind. It needed computerization and modernization but for all those years it had a loyal following. The office is located right in the heart of the business district and only a half-block from City Hall. We get business from all over the city; people walk in with deeds and contracts and all kinds of documents. In addition, the building has several lawyers and physicians and even the sheriff's office, so there are a lot of documents going around. I was fortunate that space was not terribly expensive (if my landlord is reading this you cannot hold this against me and raise my rent) and I could continue to keep it. If not for the tremendous exposure that the office allows me, I probably would have done just as well out of my home.

HOW TO APPLY FOR AN EINNUMBER("EMPLOYER IDENTIFICATION NUMBER")

An **Employer Identification Number** (EIN) is a unique identification number that is assigned to a business entity so that it can easily be identified by the Internal Revenue Service. The Employer Identification Number is commonly used by employers for the purpose of reporting taxes.

You will need an Employer Identification Number for your business. You will not be able to open a business bank account until you have one. Just follow these steps:

5. Go to the IRS EIN page (https://www.irs.gov/).

6. Scroll down to the bottom and click the link that says, "APPLY ONLINE NOW." You will find the EIN number application.

7. Click the "Begin Application" button to apply for EIN number.

8. Answer about 10-15 quick questions.

9. That's it! You just got a free EIN number.

Note: The website has restricted hours as follows:

 Hours of operation:
Monday through Friday 7 a.m. to 10 p.m. Eastern Time.

IRS INSTRUCTIONS FOR A MISPLACED EIN:

If you previously applied for and received an EIN for your business, but have since misplaced it, try any or all of the following actions to locate the number:

- Find the computer-generated notice that was issued by the IRS when you applied for your EIN. This notice is issued as a confirmation of your application for, and receipt of an EIN.

- If you used your EIN to open a bank account, or apply for any type of state or local license, you should contact the bank or agency to secure your EIN.

- Find a previously filed tax return for your existing entity (if you have filed a return) for which you have lost or misplaced EIN. Your previously filed return should be notated with your EIN.

As a last resort:

- Ask the IRS to search for your EIN by calling the Business & Specialty Tax Line at (800) 829-4933. The hours of operation are 7:00 a.m. - 7:00 p.m. local time, Monday through Friday. An assistant will ask you for identifying information and provide the number to you over the telephone, as long as you are a person who is authorized to receive it. Examples of an authorized person include but are not limited to, a sole proprietor, a partner in a partnership, a corporate officer, a trustee of a trust, or an executor of an estate.

WARNING: THERE IS NO ALTERNATIVE TO GETTING AN EIN NUMBER; YOU NEED ONE TO OPEN A CHECKING ACCOUNT AND TO PAY TAXES.

SHOULD YOU REGISTER YOUR BUSINESS AS A MINORITY?

Let's begin with the definition of a Minority Owned Business ("MBE"). Ownership by minority individuals means the business is at least 51% owned by such individuals or, in the case of a publicly-owned business, at least 51% of the stock is owned by one or more such individuals. Further, the management and daily operations are controlled by those minority group members. According to the U.S. Small Business Administration, minorities own more than 4.1 million firms and account for nearly $700 billion in revenues.

MBE's can be self-identified.

A **Minority Business Enterprise** (MBE) is an American term that is defined as a business which is at least 51% owned, operated and controlled on a daily basis by one or more (in combination) American citizens of the following ethnic minority and/or gender (e.g. woman-owned) and/or military veteran classifications:

1. Women-Owned Businesses

2. African American

3. Asian American (includes West Asian Americans (India, etc.) and East Asian Americans (Japan, Korea, etc.))

4. Hispanic American - Persons with origins from Latin America, South America, Portugal, and Spain (SBA.gov)

5. Native American including Aleuts

6. Service-Disabled Veteran-Owned a.k.a. SDVBE, a.k.a. DVBE* which became a federally certified classification in 1999, subsequent to the passage of legislation by the United States Congress through the enactment of The Veterans Entrepreneurship and Small Business Act of 1999 (The Act); legislation that was further expanded by Congress in 2001.

THE BENEFITS OF BEING A MINORITY-OWNED BUSINESS WITH CERTIFICATION

The process of becoming certified as a minority-owned business for the purposes of participating in special programs like those offered by the NMSDC (National Minority Supplier Development Council) and the SBA's 8 (Small Business Administration) (a) are significant, but the benefits of being a minority-owned business with certification is significant too. From federal and government agencies to private corporations, there are many organizations that want to do business with minority-owned businesses and would even prefer to do so. Certification may provide businesses with opportunities for which it might not otherwise, be able to compete.

Many federal government agencies are even mandated to reward a substantial number of contracts to certified minority-owned businesses. For example, the U.S. Department of Transportation requires that at least 10 percent of the money spent on contracts for certain projects go to businesses that are minority-owned, and entities (such as state transportation agencies) that receive DOT funding are required to develop Disadvantaged Business Enterprise (DBE) programs to ensure compliance.

7 BENEFITS TO BECOMING CERTIFIED AS A MINORITY-OWNED BUSINESS:

https://www.allbusiness.com/7-benefits-becoming-certified-minority-owned-business-98020-1.html

23

CHOOSINGANACCOUNTANT

Before you meet with an accountant, do some research and be prepared with a list of questions. As we said earlier, you must consult the experts, but keep in mind this is your business and you need to make the final decisions that you feel will be best for you and your business. You might want to ask for some references. Make sure you feel comfortable talking to your accountant, and that you believe that he or she has your best interest at heart 100%.

ASK YOUR ACCOUNTANT

Now you have chosen an accountant. There are some decisions that initially need to be made. Should you form an LLC or an S corporation? Are you considering a Partnership? Should your business be cash or accrual? Sit down with your new accountant and talk it through.

Below are brief descriptions of some of the avenues you might travel.

LIMITED LIABILITY COMPANY

Simply put, a Limited Liability Corporation ("LLC") is the least complex business structure. Like an s Corp or c Corp, the structure of an LLC is flexible. Starting an LLC also gives you the perk of pass-through taxes, limited liability (obviously), and legal protection for your personal assets.

For many small business owners, an LLC offers advantages over a **C corporation** (also known as a "general" **corporation**). Creating an LLC combines the tax advantages of a sole proprietorship or partnership with the **liability** protection of a **corporation**.

S CORPORATION

New corporations, as well as **LLC,'s** considering corporate taxation can choose between filing taxes as a C corporation ("C Corp") or an S corporation ("S Corp"). An S Corp is considered a "pass-through entity," which means the business itself isn't taxed. Instead, income is reported on the owners' personal tax returns.

C CORPORATION

A C corporation is a business term that is used to distinguish this type of entity from others, as its profits are taxed separately from its owners under subchapter C of the Internal Revenue Code. In an S corporation, the profits are passed on to the shareholders and are taxed based on personal returns.

PARTNERSHIP

A Partnership is a legal form of business operation between two or more individuals who share management and profits. The federal government recognizes several types of partnerships. The two most common are general and limited partnerships.

LIMITED PARTNERSHIPS

A *Limited Partnership* is a *partnership* consisting of a general partner, who manages the business and has unlimited personal liability for the debts and obligations of the *Limited Partnership*, and a *limited* partner, who has *limited* liability but cannot participate in management.

Business partners often start businesses together with little planning and few ground rules. Sooner or later, they discover the hard way that what's left unsaid or unplanned often leads to unmet expectations, anger, and frustration. Partners can clash over countless things, including conflicting work ethics and financial goals, roles in the business and leadership styles. What follows is a primer on how to avoid that and set up — and sustain — a business partnership.

Potential partners may want to consider taking a two- or three-day retreat together to go over their individual expectations for the business and partnership, one by one, and compare notes. It can help the conversation to have the partners guess each other's expectations before revealing them to each other.

Be especially careful when partnering with close friends or family members. Like many marriages, business partnerships can end in a bitter divorce. Consider whether you're willing to risk hurting your relationship if the partnership falls apart.

Approach a partnership with close friends or family as you might with strangers: Thoughtfully plan and prepare for every aspect of it in advance so there's no question about how difficult situations will be handled.

A note about partnering with a spouse: Working together puts an added strain on a relationship, and couples can quickly discover there is a little too much togetherness. Those who succeed often have learned to set boundaries to keep the business from dominating every aspect of their lives. For example, they may have agreed to leave the office at 5 P.M. and put all conversation about work on hold until after the kids are in bed.

Once the decision is made to start a business together, you should create a partnership agreement with help from a lawyer and an accountant. **Take this step no matter who your partner is.** People with strong personal connections may feel certain that their supposedly unbreakable bond will help them overcome any obstacles along the way. Big mistake. Write an agreement.

DO YOU NEED TO GET A BUSINESS LICENSE?

Starting a business? It's time to get cozy with government regulations. One of the first things you need to do is get the proper licenses or permits from the appropriate agencies to operate your business legally.

Remember to check your local and state guidelines.

Business licenses and permits are intended to keep consumers safe and operations transparent. The U.S. Small Business Administration says that virtually every business needs some sort of license or permit from state officials, but requirements vary based on the type of business, where it's located, and what government rules apply. If your business is involved in activities supervised and regulated by a federal agency, then you need to obtain a federal license or permit.

Look for Business License Policies Near You

It's often the case that different business licenses might be required on the state, city, and county levels. Additionally, if a board, commission, or association regulates your industry, you may be required to present a certification from those bodies before receiving a state or county business license. You'll need to be sure to check if your local government has specific business license policies related to your business.

This process can be quite taxing, but services like City Applications can help you locate licenses and permits needed across the country in specific locations. You can also, do your own sleuthing through the state-level agencies.

See our state-by-state breakdown below to help you find everything you need to get your business credentialed in no time—note that it's usually helpful to have your Taxpayer ID ready and to have registered for a Federal EIN Number to ease the process.

ALABAMA

AtlasAlabama is a statewide website established to help start and expand small businesses in the state. You can find information here about what businesses need occupational licenses, how to obtain a business tax number, and many other forms.

ALASKA

The Alaska Department of Commerce has a great breakdown for you. Check their list for businesses that don't require a license. You can file for your license online here. Note that you must renew once a year by January 1 with a $50 fee!

ARIZONA

This nifty guide is designed to help Arizona businesses comply with the state's basic tax and licensing requirements. You can apply for certain licenses online here.

ARKANSAS

Use this website to search for online license registration forms for your specific type of business in Arkansas.

CALIFORNIA

CalGold is your source for business licenses and permits in California. Simply search for your business type and follow the instructions from there.

COLORADO

The Colorado Business Express is your portal to filing for a business license both online or manually. Check here to see if your business qualifies for a license.

CONNECTICUT

Check out the state of Connecticut's New Business Checklist to go through everything you'll need in order to file for a license. Then search for your license registration forms by business type here. If you're still having trouble, they also have a 5-step "Wizard" to get you going.

DELAWARE

Go here to register or renew a Delaware business license. There, a questionnaire will lead you to the appropriate forms to obtain the license you need.

DISTRICT OF COLUMBIA

All businesses are required to have a license in D.C. and most can apply for a basic business license through this portal.

FLORIDA

You can get information on licensing requirements in Florida right here. Click on your business type and follow the instructions from there.

GEORGIA

Start here to submit an application for a new license—but be sure to check this list of license types in the state of Georgia before you begin.

HAWAII

Hawaii's Business Express automates the process of registering your business online. You need to have or create an eHawaii.gov account ahead of time.

IDAHO

You can search Idaho.gov's online services by your business type for any related license forms and instructions you need.

ILLINOIS

Applications for specific business type licenses can be found here for businesses in Illinois. You can also check out their First Stop Business Info Center to help you get started.

INDIANA

Indiana's Business Owner Guide is a great place to get the information you need to start your business, including licensing and permitting issues.

IOWA

According to <u>Iowa Economic Development</u>, Iowa does not have a general business license: "Licensing and other compliance requirements are based on the nature of a business or professional occupation. IASourceLink provides a comprehensive license search engine and personalized assistance to help identify compliance requirements."

KANSAS

To register a business in Kansas, use <u>this guide</u> to decide which structure you'd like to organize your business with. Then you can head to the <u>Kansas Business Center</u> online to finish the process.

KENTUCKY

The <u>Kentucky One Stop Business Portal</u> is designed to help your business start and succeed. You need to <u>create an account</u> on the site first.

LOUISIANA

Create an account on <u>GeauxBiz.com</u> to start the process of obtaining your license in Louisiana. You'll be prompted to start a business license checklist that will name the "resources to help plan, make key financial decisions, and complete legal activities necessary to start a business."

MAINE

According to Maine.gov, "General licenses to operate a business are managed at the town/city level in Maine. Contact your town office for information. To obtain contact information for your town office or to locate your municipal website, visit the <u>Maine.gov Local Government portal.</u>"

MARYLAND

The Maryland Department of Commerce has <u>compiled a database</u> of statewide and county level licenses you might need to operate a business. Compile a search based on your business type and structure.

MASSACHUSETTS

This <u>comprehensive database</u> of license and permit requirements needed for businesses in Massachusetts will lead you in the right direction. The site advises that you follow up with appropriate authorities to make sure the information is up to date.

MICHIGAN

Not every <u>business in Michigan</u> is required to be licensed by the state. Licenses are required for certain vocations or occupations that may be conducted within a business, and local governments may also require business licenses. Find out if your new venture could require a state license or permit through the <u>business license search</u>. And check out their <u>guidebook</u> and <u>step-by-step outline</u> for how to start a business in Michigan.

MINNESOTA

Minnesota <u>E-licensing</u> lets you search for required licenses by topic, agency, or index. Note that you do need a <u>state tax ID</u> to get your license.

MISSISSIPPI

Search this list of <u>professional licenses</u> in Mississippi and be sure to check out their <u>Business One Stop Shop</u> to get you good and started.

MISSOURI

The <u>Missouri Business Portal</u> lets you register with the Secretary of State and Department of Revenue simultaneously and provides a list of occupations that require licensing. They suggest you <u>contact</u> your county/city government to learn more about their requirements.

MONTANA

Search this <u>index of licenses</u> to find the one most suitable for your business—it will link you to the appropriate state agency that administers the license.

NEBRASKA

The Nebraska <u>Licensing Division</u> oversees collection agencies, debt management agencies, credit services organizations, private detectives, truth and deception examiners, athlete agents and nonrecourse civil litigation funding companies. Follow the links on their website to get your required license and check with your local government to see if they require additional licenses.

NEVADA

The <u>Silver Flume Business Portal</u> has a step-by-step guide to starting your business and getting appropriate licensing.

NEW HAMPSHIRE

New Hampshire has what it calls the Online Professional Licensing portal right here.

NEW JERSEY

The New Jersey Business Action Center makes it easy for you to find the state licenses and permits you need.

NEW MEXICO

You can search for required licenses and permits by county in New Mexico right here. Your business license requirements can also be compiled in a single online report in minutes.

NEW YORK

Want to find out what permits or licenses your business needs in New York? Start with the Business Wizard to determine which New York State licenses are necessary to get your business up and running.

NORTH CAROLINA

The State of North Carolina does not issue general business licenses, but your business might be subject to state, city, county, and federal requirements. Click here for a directory of all occupational boards in

N.C. and their contact information. Call the Business Link North Carolina (BLNC) team at (800) 228-8443 or (919) 447-7828 to determine your state license needs.

NORTH DAKOTA

Links to licenses you need in North Dakota can be found in this index.

OHIO

Step one in Ohio's guide to starting a business informs you of the legal structure variations involved in business licensing. You can then search this index to find the licenses you need.

OKLAHOMA

Go here for the list of Oklahoma business licenses and permits by county.

OREGON

The Oregon <u>License Directory Search</u> is the #1 spot to help you get started on your state of Oregon business licenses, permits, and registrations.

PENNSYLVANIA

<u>This list</u> is a good place to start your search for a Pennsylvania business license. Many Pennsylvania businesses are required to get some sort of operating business license or a business permit from the state of Pennsylvania or from their corresponding county or city in Pennsylvania.

RHODE ISLAND

You can find forms for business licenses in Rhode Island on their secretary of state <u>website</u>: Click on "Step 4: Find forms for your business," which will prompt a questionnaire. You can also <u>search directly</u> using keywords for your business.

SOUTH CAROLINA

The Division of Business Filings in S.C. files licensing forms for businesses, but sole proprietorships and general partnerships do not have to file with the Division. To learn more about each of these divisions, call (803) 734-2158.

SOUTH DAKOTA

This handy <u>PDF</u> has all the info you need on getting a business license in South Dakota.

TENNESSEE

According to the Tennessee Department of Revenue, if you have an in-state business with sales of more than $3,000, you must obtain either a "minimal activity license" or a "standard business license" from your county or municipal clerk. For more information, <u>click here</u>.

TEXAS

Texas has two places for registering or renewing business licenses. The Department of Licensing and Regulation has <u>this list of</u> occupations that require licenses. You can also go to Texas.gov and scroll down to the "Work" section to see more specific licenses related to your business.

UTAH

To get a business license in Utah, select your occupation or profession for this list on the state website. They'll direct you from there on out.

VERMONT

You can obtain a license for your business through the Vermont business portal here.

VIRGINIA

The Virginia.gov Business One Stop recommends looking up if your business requires a license through City Applications. You can then register quickly online through One Stop.

WASHINGTON

Use this list of licenses for Washington to determine what your business needs. You can then file for the license online by clicking on your business type.

WEST VIRGINIA

West Virginia has a licenses directory you can search right here. Though they don't guarantee they have every license listed, they recommend you check with local officials in your area.

WISCONSIN

Wisconsin's department of safety and professional services have you covered—search for your business type through their portal here.

WYOMING

Business licenses in Wyoming are provided through professional boards. See the list of boards here to check if your business needs a license.

HOW TO CHOOSE A NAME
FOR YOUR BUSINESS

Now you have given birth and you must give your baby a name. This is very personal but probably one of the most important things you need to do if you want to have a successful business. In my case I was lucky – I bought an established name in my city and a name that is reflective of success. I personally don't care for trendy names, but they work. I like a name that sounds a little serious. Let's compare: "Judi's Notaries Are the Best" it does speak, but compare it to "Center City Notary" … that name gives a more professional nuance and it sounds like you have been around for a long time and plan on staying even longer. If you are not creative, look at naming agencies like Zinzin.com. Companies like this will create a name and an image for you.

Do your research. Check out the competition in your area and see what people call their businesses.

A fun idea is to maybe have a small gathering and make it into a naming contest. Try out several names and get some opinions. Have a few people call you and answer the phone, see what it sounds like. In some instances, if it is a longer name, you might want to try shortening it. The name of my company is Center City Notary. I answer our phones using the entire name rather than CCN. I think the more people hear the name, the more they remember it.

Here are some tips–

- Although trendy is good, you need to stay away from anything religious or political. You don't want to give people a reason to say they would never use your company;

- When you hand a customer your business card, if the opportunity presents itself, tell them to be sure to save your information in their phone under **NOTARY**. A year later they may not remember your name but if they look under "notary" your contact information will be right there;

- Set up a V Card in Outlook (see chapter entitled Using Outlook) which will be attached to every email you send; and

- If you are sending an electronic receipt, make sure you have your contact information on the receipt. I don't know how many times I get an email for a quote from the receipt thread which I sent them.

WARNING: THE NAME OF YOUR BUSINESS SHOULD BE NOTHING TRENDY, RELIGIOUS, OR POLITICAL

Picking a Perfect Name
https://startupbros.com/how-to-pick-the-perfect-name-for-your-business-or- startup/

HOW TO CREATE BUSINESS CARDS

You have chosen a name, now you need a business card.

A business card is one of the most important ingredients to a successful business. It is often the last thing you give a client, and how he or she will keep a record of your information for future business. Very few people still use a Rolodex. Now, a high percentage of people take your card and when they get home or back to their own office, they scan it right into their contacts and throw the physical card away. But if it is in their contacts, the next time they need a notary, they will reach out to you.

The card needs to include:

- Your Name
- Name of Company
- Services
- Address
- Phone Number
- Fax Number
- Email
- Website

Certain states may require a disclaimer on the card that says you are not an attorney. Refer to "Tools" on our website for more information about your specific state requirements.

To start, design the card yourself and order the cards in small quantities because you will find yourself needing to make changes as your business continues to grow. It took me one year to be happy with the format and the logo and I still continuously make edits as we add services and make changes.

Keep your fonts large enough to be able to be easily read. There is nothing worse than having to squint to read a phone number.

Another thing to keep in mind— it is sometimes better to have two cards. In my business, I have a card for "notarizations" and a card for "apostilles." Apostilles are very specialized and I found that when I was pitching that kind of work, telling people I could do them, but handing them a card all about notaries, it was not working for me. I created a second company that has its own business card and sometimes I pass along both cards when appropriate.

I would recommend Vista Print (www.vistaprint.com) for personalized business cards. Their prices are good, and they are helpful and most importantly they are user-friendly.

NEVER GIVE OUT A BUSINESS CARD WITH A TYPO. This is very important. It reflects who you are, and although people may not say anything, they will notice. They will ask themselves: if you don't pay attention to your business card, what will you do with their work?

7 Tips on What to Put on Your Business Card: https://business.tutsplus.com/articles/7-tips-on-what-information-to-put-on-your-business-card--cms-25194

10 Business Card Mistakes You Might Be Making: https://archive.ama.org/.../10-Business-Card-Mistakes-You-Might-be-Making.aspx

HOW TO PURCHASE
A DOMAIN NAME(S)

Before you definitely decide on a name and business cards, you need to make sure that name does not belong to anyone else and then you need to make sure that no one else can copy the name.

You can go to the corporation bureau of your specific state and see if anyone is using the name. The last thing you want to do is select a name, order cards, start working on a website only to find that the name is already registered to someone else.

Once you know the name is available, the company I suggest you use to purchase a domain name is www.godaddy.com. Their telephone number is (480) 505-8877. Their customer service is A+, they are available 24/7 and they will walk you through the process. They also have very competitive pricing.

Now, if your company is going to be called Best Notary, you might want to consider also purchasing Best Notaries and then perhaps Best Notaries. com if those similar names are available.

A website and other online situations will not work unless connected to a legitimate domain name, so be sure you take care of getting this in place even if you are not planning to use it for 3-6 months while you are setting up.

Go-Daddy will email you or call you when these domain names must be renewed.

SOME TECHNICAL DETAILS:

Domain names are used to identify one or more *IP addresses*. For example, the domain name *microsoft.com* represents about a dozen IP addresses. Domain names are used in URLs to identify particular web pages. For example, in the URL *http://www.pcwebopedia.com/index.html,* the domain name is *pcwebopedia.com*.

Every domain name has a suffix that indicates which top-level domain (TLD) it belongs to. There are only a limited number of such domains. For example:

- **gov** - Government agencies
- **edu** - Educational institutions
- **org** - Organizations (nonprofit)
- **mil** - Military
- **com** - Commercial business
- **net** - Network organizations
- **ca** - Canada

Because the Internet is based on IP addresses, not domain names, every web server requires a Domain Name System (DNS) server to translate domain names into IP addresses.

HOW TO SELECT YOUR LOGO

Make this a fun experience. There are lots of graphic and imaging sites on the Internet. Get some input from friends and family. Your logo will be with you for a long time – it will be on your business card, your website, letterhead, marketing materials, invoices and materials you develop along the way. I personally like colors that POP, but some people prefer a plainer, more classic look. There is one important thing to keep in mind—you should try to stay with what you pick; through your logo, your company becomes branded; people recognize the brand and that's good for business.

When you are starting your business, you might want to check out www. vistaprint.com. They give you a large selection of logos that you can upload directly into your business cards. In my case, my business took directions that I never would have thought of, and my cards and my logo continuously changed until I was completely sure. Vistaprint allows you to make those changes at a lower cost than having it all professionally re-designed.

You might also like www.pixabay.com, a free site for interesting logos and graphics.

ALL ABOUT BRANDING

BusinessDictionary.com defines branding as:

> "The process involved in creating a unique name and image for a product in the consumer's mind, mainly through advertising campaigns with a consistent theme. Branding aims to establish a significant and differentiated presence in the market that attracts and retains loyal customers."

(Read more at http:/www.businessdictinary.com/definition/branding.html.)

We have all seen forms of branding for many years. For example, the Golden Arches is the rand we all recognize as McDonalds; and the jingle "Like a Good Neighbor" (originally written by Barry Manilow) will always be is State Farm. Sometimes the company changes their music, their message or their array of services, but they never change that logo which we all immediately have recognized for years.

Whether your business becomes a large one or you decide to keep it small, when you finally decide on a logo, I suggest you make it something you LOVE and try to stay with it. I recently changed my colors, but my actual logo remains the same. It is on my website, business cards, invoices, letterhead, checks, and on all my marketing pieces including my brochures.

DO NOT PUT ALL YOUR EGGS IN ONE BASKET

Starting a new business is all-encompassing. In the beginning you need to focus on one thing— getting a protocol or a model in place for whatever you are doing and making sure you have quality control set up so that you are delivering a high-quality finished product. Take a few months to get this all-in place. Getting the right equipment and paying attention to the zillion other small details will make the business both efficient and profitable.

Once you are comfortable, take stock of what you are doing and what else you can do to generate additional revenue.

In my case, I started with a notary company which today, in addition to notaries, does mobile notary closings, apostilles and auto tags.

So, let's say you decide to open a knit shop. You might begin with needles and wool and some patterns. What about adding a class for people who want to learn to knit? Or one-on-one training for those who are uncomfortable in a classroom environment? You might be surprised to find that your revenue for the training exceeds your revenue for the needles, wool, and patterns. You might also consider crocheting. You could develop a whole new division of your knit shop for crocheting. We live in a world of TRENDS and you must make sure that your business is expandable enough to catch the trends. If the knit division of your business drops off because everyone is suddenly crocheting, you survive. Get the point?

The Benefits of Diversifying Your Business: https://www.santandercb. co.uk/insight-and-events/news/benefits-diversification

LANDLINE VS. WIRELESS?

This is a big decision.

For me there was no decision; my business needed to be wireless.

Of course, wireless is far less expensive and that is always a consideration. But I had a vision. My office is located right in the heart of the business district. We are surrounded by office buildings and hotels. My vision was to tell everyone who would listen that if it was 7:00 A.M. or 9:00 P.M., our company would answer the phone and be available to assist. The only way to do that, aside from moving into my little office, was to have the phone be wireless, and as they say, where it goeth, I goeth. (Not sure if they really say that, but you get my drift.)

And before you say a word, I could have used a landline and just used call forwarding, but it seemed easier and more reliable to just be wireless. For me, it has worked out extraordinarily well. I have my phone and no matter where I am or what time it is, I can answer a call, give a quote and in some instances, get to a hospital room or another location within a few minutes.

But I want to be clear and say that THIS WOULD NOT WORK FOR EVERYONE. You must be a person who does not consider this an intrusion. I am writing this topic on the afternoon of Christmas Eve and so far, today I have had a hotel and a hospital emergency signing. Most importantly, you must be a person who can "spin on a dime." And, again, you need to take into consideration whether you have a spouse or a partner or a significant other, or you are a mom or a dad. An answering service might be a better way for you.

I have an iPhone 8. I am aware that iPhones (or any cellular phones for that matter) can just stop working and usually, it takes a day (or two) to get the phone replaced. I solved that problem by getting myself an iPhone 7. That phone is a mirror of my 8. It usually sits in my drawer, but in an emergency, I would have a phone until my primary phone could be replaced.

I must stress that you need to back up your phone every day. This takes two minutes. The worst thing that could happen is that you have entered that very important new client's contact information in your phone and you need to follow up next week, but something happens, your data is not backed up, and the information is lost for good.

Here is a very informative article on the Pros and Cons of wireless vs. landline:

Pros and Cons of Switching a Business Phone landline to wireless: http://smallbusiness.chron.com/pros-cons-switching-business-phone-land-line-cellular-80442.html

ALL ABOUT SMARTPHONES

I Finally Realized That People Are Prisoners of Their Phones and That's Why It's Called a Cell Phone.

Remember that old expression, **THE BUCK STOPS HERE**? Well, it may be an old expression but in 2018 it is relevant. If you do not already have one, you will need a smartphone to conduct business. Even if you have regular hours, as the owner of the business you will need to be available **ALL THE TIME**. Contingent upon your business, and no matter if you are fortunate enough to have the best assistant in the world, you are the one who is responsible whether there is a heating problem, a job cannot be delivered on time or a job is delivered to the wrong client. IT IS ALL ABOUT YOU.

So, your question might be: "What will the smartphone do for me? And the answer is "Everything."

Here are some examples of what I mean:

ANSWERING THE PHONE

Okay, I have a confession to make. I am the operator who answers my phone. Are you looking at me like I am crazy? I answer the phone because in the world of press 1, press 2 and press 3, people like to hear a human voice. My company is 24/7. I sometimes get calls at 11:00 P.M about one document to notarize that they don't need until the next day. But they do want to hear a voice, get the price, the address, and the availability. Sometimes someone calls about a one-page affidavit, and sometimes that call is about a complex 4:00 A.M. signing.

EMAIL

You will need to be able to access your email on your phone. Believe me, when you are out and about and away from your computer, whether personally or professionally, being able to access your email will make money for you. Whatever business you decide to start, there is competition on the Internet. In my notary business, for example, I often get emails asking for quotes. I don't delude myself; they are sending three emails to three different competitors. In many instances, the first one to respond wins the prize. You will also want to keep in touch with customers, answer a quick question, or at least let them know that you acknowledge the question and will respond as soon as you get back to the office.

TEXTING

More and more clients use texting as a platform to communicate with their database of professional notaries. Clients often use texting, more so than calling, to get a message out to a group of people. They use texting for looking up health information, online banking, checking real estate listings, seeking new employees, downloading job applications, obtaining driving directions, announcing assignments, posting compensation, and getting rapid responses to better serve their clients. They ask for a quote and your availability and yes, even if your hours are posted on your website, they still text you with questions. The quicker you respond, the more you increase the chance of getting that business and therefore increasing your income.

CONTACTS

You will have your contacts with you. If you are diligent about saving them, you will always have access to your landlord, customers, and vendors for that emergency that may happen when you are not in the office. Your phone will act as your "little black book" and you will be portable no matter where you are or what time it is. Having that number easily accessible can make the difference.

CALENDAR

You will have your appointments accessible. As you will read in the chapter entitled "How and Why to Use Outlook," you will find that if you don't keep your appointments online, when you are sitting in that important meeting and everyone begins talking about a date for the next meeting, you will probably be the only one who will say "I have to go back and check my calendar and I will get back to you."

NOTIFICATIONS AND ALERTS

This will be one of the most valuable tools in your toolbox on your smartphone. You can set up alerts on your phone. Using this, you will not be late and, heaven forbid, miss an appointment. For example, if you have a signing on January 4, you might set up an alert for January 2 to follow up and see if you have received the documents, and then again on January 4 to make sure you leave in plenty of time to not be late. It is bad business to be late for anything.

ANSWERING PHONES

If you are starting any kind of service business and you want it to take off, you need to answer the phones. Now you scratched your head and said to yourself, "What is she talking about? Everyone answers the phone when it rings." But that is not what I meant. In the beginning and for a long time, you need to be the one to answer the phone when others do not, such as evenings and weekends. I have built a strong business by making sure to almost never miss a call.

Why is this so important? Because we live in a world of immediate gratification. I began a notary business and I wanted (and still want) to capture every customer that I possibly can.

FACT: when a prospective customer calls for a notary and gets a machine, he or she calls the next notary online.

And FACT: sometimes (especially on a weekend) they call 10 or 12 places until someone answers the phone. So, I made myself available and got most of the work after business hours and over the weekends.

ONE MORE FACT: once a customer is happy with your service, and knows that you are always available, they will wait for you. (I say this because a lot of my wonderful customers will read this book and I want you all to know how grateful I am for all the times you waited for me.)

I have picked up signings including one at 4:00 A.M. and lots of deed packages for which clients were available only after 7:00 P.M. I have physicians who are available only after 9:00 P.M. and athletes who come into town and need something notarized within the hour. These are now my clients whom I believe will be loyal to me and will wait for me, but had no one answered the phone, in all probability that business would have gone elsewhere.

Let me also add that sometimes it is not the biggest job in the world, often someone will call at 8:00 PM and all they want to know is will someone be there in the morning. But in my experience, that "hands-on" approach wins in the end.

It is very simple; if you choose to have a landline in your office, just use call forwarding and watch your calls and your business come flooding in.

Co-author Daniel C. Lewis adds the following:

It is not just important that you answer the phone, but how you answer the phone is also important. When I first started as a notary signing agent I found very quickly that I received more repeat business by answering the phone on the **first ring**. Because people are busy when they call you, if your phone tends to ring repeatedly and is not answered until the third or fourth ring, they tend to hang up and start calling someone else. This is particularly true with busy schedulers who just want to get a job scheduled and move on to the next one.

CUSTOMER SERVICE
– OR LACK OF IT

"I don't know that there are any shortcuts to doing a good job"

–Justice Sandra Day O'Connor

> SUCCESS IS
> NEVER OWNED,
> IT IS RENTED.
> AND THE RENT
> IS DUE EVERY
> DAY.

I want to share a few short stories about customer service or lack of it. In 2018, to be successful, and to pay that rent every day, you need to have more than excellent customer service.

Truth told, most service business people answer their phones 24/7, and often they are somewhere other than the office. The first time I saw this was 7 or 8 years ago while playing blackjack in a casino in Las Vegas. The man on my right was doing a deal while he was playing. I am #1 at doing that (not playing blackjack and working, but answering my phones 24/7). I answer EVERY CALL, and as I said earlier, I pick up many interesting and profitable jobs by doing so.

We live in a world where everyone is looking for immediate gratification—people have a mile-long to-do list and they want to get as many items checked off as quickly as possible.

So, a few examples of how to lose business . . .

One Sunday I found myself in need of a courier. I went online and searched for a courier available 24/7 and called the first one. A very nice-sounding woman answered the phone. I told her what I needed. She said, "Honey, I am in the supermarket. Give me about 45 minutes to finish up and once I get home, I will look at my price list, and I will check and see if I have anyone available and I will call you back." Of course, by the time she called me back, my courier was on the way.

How should you handle that? First, it is not important to let anyone know where you are. If you are in a restaurant or in the supermarket, find a quiet corner and do business. Second, always carry your price list because 99% of the time, the price will be a deal vs. a deal-breaker. And third, always know who is available; you should have names and numbers in your contacts on your phone and a schedule (if applicable) in your pocket.

Recently I was hosting a charity event on a Wednesday in my office and I needed 10 bags of ice which I needed to have delivered. Unless you are looking for 75 bags of ice, this is practically impossible. Finally, I connected with someone who said they could do it. The price was good, and I offered to give her my credit card and my delivery information, to which she replied, "That's okay, call me on Wednesday morning and we can get it there for you." Of course, I hung up and found someone else.

How should you handle that? She should have locked me in, taken my card, and clinched the deal. I could have called there Wednesday morning and she was no longer there, or out that day, and a new person would have no clue and maybe no ice.

One day I had to call a printer about a 5,000-page job. I called someone in my neighborhood and he said, "Hey, I don't know a thing about that, but if you call back at 10:30, someone might be here who can go over that with you."

How should you handle that? We live in a world of cell phones and 5,000 pages is a lot of pages. I would have put the customer on hold, called someone (maybe even the boss), and got us hooked up. Remember, he would have probably gotten not only that job but print jobs that I might have in the future.

IF YOU DID NOT WRITE IT, YOU DID NOT SAY IT AND IF YOU DID WRITE IT, YOU'D BEST DO IT.

"The future rewards those who press on. I don't have time to feel sorry for myself. I don't have time to complain. I'm going to press on."

—President Barack Obama

With email being our dominant means of communication, people have become used to the immediate "confirmation." You order something online and within minutes a confirmation appears, and if it does not, you know that something went wrong. Make an airline reservation and you will have a confirmation in seconds.

So, let's look at this as a business owner. You will need to remember the golden rule—**If You Did Not Write It, You Did Not Say It, and If You Did Write It, You'd Best Do It.**

Here is an example:

Notary A gets a call from a hotel. A large board meeting will be taking place on a specific Sunday. They will need three notaries to be present from 8:00 AM to 6:00 PM. Julie, the owner of Notary A, quotes them a price, taking into consideration that she will need to have additional staff available. The hotel is pleased with the quote and the job is booked. <u>Julie does not send a written (email) confirmation.</u>

Next, the owner of Notary B gets the same call from the hotel. Nancy, the owner of Notary B gives them a slightly less expensive quote and adds that they will bring a portable scanner to the meeting. The hotel is more than pleased and books the job. <u>Nancy immediately sends the hotel an email</u> confirming everything they spoke about and she requests that the hotel confirm the booking via an email. <u>The hotel confirms the appointment</u> via email and they are all set.

The hotel does not even bother to call Notary A to cancel.

On that Sunday Julie and her group arrive at the hotel to be told they already have notaries onsite. Julie has no leg to stand on. She did <u>almost</u> everything right, but she did not write it and has no confirmation that she even said it. Julie lost one day's business, not to mention having to pay her other two notaries.

Be very sure that most people are saving your emails (Outlook folders in the previous chapter make this a simple thing to do) and remember – if you did not write it, you did not say it, and if you did write it, you'd best do it.

INVOICING

No matter what business you decide to start, your invoicing is one of the critical ingredients to your success. Keeping track of what you made, what you spent, and what people owe you is essential.

If you are just going to be a notary signer, you don't need anything with lots of bells and whistles. I started out with InvoiceASAP (invoiceasap. com). It was a good tracking system. I was able to access it on my phone, which was convenient. But as we continued to grow, I needed more, and I changed to QuickBooks. Although learning it is difficult, once you get used to it, it is very user-friendly and gives you and your accountant all the numbers that are necessary. (www.quickbooks.com)

Another good feature is that you can email invoices; not only is that quicker, but people actually keep the receipts and sometimes that is how they retain your contact information.

In addition to Quick Books being an excellent system, for me, this acts as my database. I know how many transactions I have done, and I have a record of the names, addresses, and emails of all my customers.

Lewis Notary Service Inc.
681 Helen Keen Court
Carmel, IN 46032
Tel: 317 403 1282 Fax: 317 815 4869
admin@lewisnotary.com

Invoice

Invoice #:	1770
Invoice Date:	03/04/2018
Customer ID:	106369
Terms:	

Bill To:	Borrower:
Center City Notary **100 S Broad Street Flr 14** **Philadelphia, PA 19110** **2158703103**	Judith Lawrence Judith Lawrence 123 Acme Street Philadelphia, PA 19110

Reference Information:

Request#: 1,868   Signing Date: 03/05/2018   Loan/Escrow#: 123345

This invoice was emailed to centercitynotary100@gmail.com on 3/4/2018.

Qty	Description	Unit Price	Price
1	Notary	100.00	100.00
	Thank You, Loan Officer Name: Loan Officer Phone: Tracking Number:		
	(P)171-(0)118/400- (R)1653675	**Sub Total**	100.00
		Other	0.00
		Total	100.00

PAY PAL

Coronavirus has definitely moved us closer and closer to contactless (and cashless) payment options. Technology is making life easier and harder at the same time. With Amazon, Walmart, and other vendors making it easier and easier to do contactless transactions notaries can take advantage of this new technology. Contactless is the fastest, easiest and safest, and as of late, as announced by the World Health Organization, the healthiest way to pay.

Notaries can receive contactless payments in a variety of different ways. Many companies use e-checks along with other methods of contactless payment options. Here are just a few contactless payment options:

eCHECKS using DELUXE PAYMENT EXCHANGE - This is an option that many vendors are turning to in order to pay notaries for their services. This option allows your customers to send your payments in seconds and reduce their expenses.

Paypal - This option allows you to receive credit card payments along with a check or cash payments. Notaries can instantly send their customers receipts which works well with general notary work customers.

Cashapp - This option allows you to send and receive money with anyone, donate to an important cause or tip professionals. Just enter a $cashtag, phone number, or scan their QR code to pay.

Venmo - Another great option. Send money and make purchases at approved merchants. Venmo also allows you to move money easily to your bank account.

Convenience is now a hot commodity in this pandemic world. Given the increased security, speed, and touch-free world that we live in now contactless payment options are here to stay.

ACCEPTING CREDIT CARDS

In the year 2020, to thrive, most businesses need to accept credit cards. A high percentage of people (including yours truly) work with credit cards.

As with any vendor, it is important that you do some research and familiarizes yourself with their products and services. <u>I made a huge mistake because I did not ask the right questions</u>. Once I knew what I wanted and what I needed and most importantly what would be affordable for my business, I was stuck in a two-year contract with the wrong vendor. If I wanted to terminate that contract I would have had to pay $790.00.

So, before you sign a contract to set up your business to be able to accept credit cards, it is critical that you do your research and be prepared to ask the right questions:

1. The length of the contract;
2. The penalty if you need to terminate;
3. The interest rate per transaction if the card is present;
4. The interest rate per transaction if the card is not present;
5. What kind of technical support is available.

You also might want to look at Square and Venmo; both are popular, both are free and both work well.

DOCUMENTING PASSWORDS AND SERIAL NUMBERS

One of the most time-consuming tasks of running your business is the time it takes to connect with vendors. The main reason is that NO ONE ANSWERS THE PHONE. You will be greeted with a list of prompts and then, when you finally get a live person, if you do not have the right credentials, you will not get the help you need. Comcast (my internet carrier) does not have my account number; they say they cannot access it. Microsoft has a long number associated with Word 365 and without it, you can hold for a month. Keep in mind that the people answering these calls have a script they follow and if you cannot provide them with your information you will more than likely be told to call back.

I strongly suggest that from day one you keep a separate document with passwords, account numbers, and serial numbers. I keep this document both at home, in the office, and, of course, in a folder on my phone.

Recently I took my first vacation in over three years. I spent five days in London. When I got a text that we were having a phone issue, I was able to call, give them the appropriate account information and I got the problem resolved.

So, you ask – why couldn't someone at the office just call and get the issue resolved? It would be a logical question. The answer is that Verizon requires that you appoint a person they can speak to in your absence. This must be put in writing and made part of their record. Failure to do so means that they will not speak to ANYONE except you.

Start your document right away. Record serial numbers of the products you buy, keep your EIN numbers and your PINs and passwords. It will save you hours of wasted time, tears, and frustration. You should keep this document in a secure, fireproof place. If you keep it on your computer keep it password protected.

I also suggest that periodically you give a copy of the document (you will continue to update) to someone you trust to take care of things in the event you cannot.

EXAMPLE:

New LG Television
Serial #1234 8765 1234
Product #1234
Customer Support: 215-999-2468
Access Code: 4567
Date of Purchase: 5.1.16
Warranty Expiration: 5.1.17

DEVELOPING AN
EFFECTIVE WEBSITE

We all know that in 2020 it is difficult, if not impossible, to imagine a business without a website. The majority of people, young or old, now go online to search for whatever they want or need. This subject could take up this entire book, as there are so many aspects to building and maintaining a website. Your website reflects who you are, your vision of your company, and your services.

I confess, I did my first website myself. I thought it was beautiful and could not have been prouder. But as time went by and my business expanded, I knew it was time to have a professionally designed website. When I saw my first professionally designed website, I clearly remember saying to my webmaster that I was pretty sure I would not need to make changes for a long time and he replied, "Yes, you will," and he was correct. Besides cost, there are many things to consider when you are deciding on a website.

From the time you create your business you will receive emails from web designers offering to help you. When you find someone that you like, you will need to ask for some websites that he or she has created and make sure that the feel is what you like. But in addition to skills, it is critical that the person that you decide to work with needs to "get you" and "get your business" and he or she needs to take a personal interest in your success.

When you take on a new project or add a new service, the first line is to change up the website so people will know what you are doing. A webmaster may understand how to create a website and know how Google works but you are the expert in your business, not the webmaster. As such, the website needs to service the unique needs of your company.

Your webmaster can be a guide, but you are, ultimately, responsible for what your website does to improve your business. From what type of website you use to what types of marketing tools you use, it is based on what your actual needs and goals are. It's the classic 'Don't put the cart in front of the horse.' Know what you want and then find the best way to get it. It's important to know your 'sweet spot'. Your 'sweet spot' is the place where you can rank the best for your particular product or service. You determine this in three major ways:

- Know what words your potential clients are actually using to search for your product or service, not what you think they might be using. Google has a keyword tool that tells you what words people are actually searching on. You OWN your keyword list; that means that you know what terms people are actually using and then you KNOW how you are ranking for those keywords.

- Know what combination of tools will work best to convert website visitors into leads. Will social media work? What about a newsletter or online forms? Do you have something you could give away to get someone's email? (That's called a lead magnet.)

- Investigate and know what your competition is doing and then do just a bit better. Google is your friend. Google is the #1 most visited site in the world. They are a great directory•Know what words your potential clients are actually using to search for your product or service, not what you think they might be using. Google has a keyword tool that tells you what words people are actually searching on. You OWN your keyword list; that means that you know what terms people are actually using and then you KNOW how you are ranking for those keywords.

- Know what combination of tools will work best to convert website visitors into leads. Will social media work? What about a newsletter or online forms? Do you have something you could give away to get someone's email? (That's called a lead magnet.)

- Investigate and know what your competition is doing and then do just a bit better. Google is your friend. Google is the #1 most visited site in the world. They are a great directory

BEST PRACTICES

Best Practices can mean many things. I have a set of Best Practices for my own business—I try to provide exemplary customer service and anyone who works for me must do the same. I also try to give a client MORE than what he or she is expecting. For example, when I notarize an agreement, I explain why I am asking them to sign in blue ink (so that it will always be original despite faxing and photocopying). I also ask them to initial the bottom right-hand corner of the document. I explain that if anyone were to try to substitute a page, this would make it more difficult, if not impossible. My state does not require a seal but we use the seal so the document looks more official. If we make a mistake, we pay for it – my goal is that everyone leaves our office and is satisfied and refers us to their friends and family. That is my personal best practice.

But as a notary, we follow the best practices set for notaries in the United States. Below is a link you will want to study and sometimes refer to when you have a question. You will find answers to many questions as to what is expected of you.

The Notary Public Code of Professional Responsibility:
https://www.nationalnotary.org/file%20library/nna/reference-library/notary_code.pdf

REVIEWS

The truth, the whole truth, and nothing but the truth: you get a high percentage of business based upon your reviews. The average person who needs something goes to Google, initiates a search, and reads the reviews.

I'm going to take the negative before the positive; no matter how good you are, and how nice you are, and no matter how hard you try, occasionally someone comes in who is either unhappy or angry, not at you but at something or someone, and he or she will write a negative review. It can be hurtful, but my advice is to concentrate on the many people who have written those excellent reviews.

Daniel told me about a negative review he received.

> Daniel went to a home for a refinance transaction. The gentleman (who we will call Jim) answered the door and was already extremely agitated. When Daniel asked Jim for his photo ID he was further agitated. When Daniel presented the closing documents to Jim his name was spelled wrong, which further upset him. The CD showed that Jim owed money and that too was upsetting because he thought he was getting a distribution. Jim said, "This company is making me sign these documents." Daniel asked if he could elaborate on exactly how he was being forced to sign the documents. Daniel explained to Jim that if he (Jim) was being coerced into signing the documents, he (Daniel) would not be allowed to notarize the documents.
>
> Jim then stood up and demanded that Daniel get out of his house. Daniel left and advised the title company immediately. The title company made all the necessary corrections and engaged Daniel to return to complete the signing, which he did.

A few months later when Daniel got a call from another company who said they wanted to use him because of a negative review Jim had left about him. What the review stated was that after Daniel told him he could not notarize the documents if coercion was involved, he asked Daniel to leave his home. It was Jim's understanding that the notary is just supposed to stamp a document and because Daniel would not do that Jim wrote this negative review which ultimately led Daniel into obtaining more business from a company that respected him for knowing right from wrong.

So how do you get those wonderful reviews? I often work on weekends and people call me a "lifesaver" and tell me about this wonderful service. I sometimes think that is what I should have named my company. We live in a fast-paced world; you provide this wonderful service, but human nature is that once the service is provided, people move on to something else. Here are a few suggestions:

First, no one ever leaves my office without my card. They say thank you for such wonderful service and in many instances, I say, "If you have a moment, would you mind going on the Internet and giving me a good review? That is how I get my business." Everyone responds and says "absolutely," but only a few actually do it.

Second, you need a link on your website where they can click and write a review. That is easy. They have your card and sometimes they will go home or to their office and do it.

If it is a large job and you want to be sure to get something, email the person that day and ask if they would be so inclined to send an email with their thoughts on how easy it was to work with the company. If it is a corporate executive, they will usually prefer that.

Also, you might want to set up your Facebook page to accept reviews.

TAKE A MOMENT AND GIVE BACK

I have always believed that giving back is an important part of life. And in business that is no exception. I encourage anyone reading this book to get involved in whatever way you like, be it your community, a charity, or an organization that you feel is important. If, in the beginning, your budget is tight, there is always a way. For example, Center City Notary is a supporter of Women Against Abuse. We do so by not charging the organization a fee for notary services.

We are also a supporter of Alex's Lemonade Stand. Once a year, we set up outside our building for an entire day and sell lemonade to benefit research for children's cancer. This will be our third year and each year we sell a little more. It is gratifying and from a business perspective, we meet a lot of people who not only support this wonderful cause but become our regular customers.

Daniel and I encourage you to feel free to email us at MakeYourBusinessOurBusiness@gmail.com and send us a photo of something you do for others. We will post the photos on our website. It is a great way for us to all get to know each other.

INTERESTING ABOUT NOTARIES
FACT OR FICTION?

Thanks to the Internet, the National Notary Association, and the American Association of Notaries for these interesting facts about notaries from various sources. (We cannot validate some of these facts since some of them originated many years ago.)

We include them so that anyone considering becoming a notary will have a concept of just how serious this is, and just how much history is behind becoming a notary public. Your commission is valuable, and you must observe and obey the policies of this charge, so you can keep it for a long time.

The word "notary" comes from the Latin word "nota," a system of shorthand developed by M. Tullius Tiro (103-3 B.C.), the clerk of Cicero. Tiro used nota to take down Cicero's speeches. People employed to receive instructions for the drafting of agreements, conveyances, and other types of instruments adopted this method of writing, and the term "notarius" was used to describe them.

Notary of The Bedchamber. In the Middle Ages, notaries were sometimes asked to witness the consummation of marriages involving royalty or members of the peerage.

They Didn't Trust Columbus. Notaries accompanied Columbus on all of his voyages just as they accompanied nearly all early Spanish explorers. The reason: King Ferdinand and Queen Isabella wanted to ensure that

Make Your Business Our Business all discovered treasures were accounted for. On October 12, 1492, when Columbus first beheld the New World, a notary named Rodrigo de Escobedo was on hand to document the landing on San Salvador Island in the Bahamas.

The first **Notary Public Day** was celebrated on November 7, 1975, and created to "recognize notaries for their public service and their contributions to national and international commerce." The date of November 7 was chosen as Notary Public Day in recognition of the day that America's first notary, Thomas Fugill, was appointed. Fugill's appointment by the Colony of New Haven occurred on October 25, 1639 (Julian calendar), November 7 on the Gregorian calendar now in use. This is celebrated every year on November 7.

Breakfast of Champions. When Wheaties executives asked baseball player Pete Rose to appear on a Wheaties box, he had to sign and swear in the presence of a notary that he'd eaten the cereal ever since he was a kid.

Draw, Mister! At one time in Tennessee, statutes forbade "known duelists" from becoming notaries because they were considered individuals of questionable reputation.

Breach of Faith. In South Carolina, a 127-year-old law requires all notary applicants to swear allegiance to God. In a case currently before the state's Supreme Court, an atheist is challenging this requirement.

Don't Get In His Way. In the classic Hollywood film, "D.O.A.," the hero played by Edmund O'Brien was a notary who had two hours to find an antidote to a deadly poison.

Get Real. Although his father wanted him to follow in his footsteps and become a notary, surrealist painter Salvador Dali had other aspirations.

Oh, My Papa! Artist-inventor Leonardo da Vinci was also the son of a notary. To safeguard his ideas, da Vinci perfected the skill of writing backwards; one must use a mirror to read his thoughts. Good thing he didn't follow in his father's footsteps.

Mark His Words. In 1864, Samuel Clemens (a.k.a. Mark Twain) became a notary public in Nevada — the only genuine public office to which he was ever appointed. The literary world is ever grateful he chose not to remain in public service.

Notarygate. Frank DeMarco, Jr., a California tax attorney and notary was accused of fraudulently backdating forms relating to former President Richard M. Nixon's donation of papers to the National Archives to beat a tax deduction deadline. After months of controversy, DeMarco resigned his notary office in June of 1970 to forestall an investigation by the state. Evidence of the alleged transaction was sent to the Watergate Special Prosecutor and was but one more incident eroding Nixon's political support and leading to his resignation from office.

Suffering Suffragettes. Not only could women not vote, but, until the early 1900s, women in America were also prohibited from becoming notaries. U.S. Supreme Court Justice Oliver Wendell Holmes Jr. held that since there was no record of women holding the office in England, it could not be affirmed that women were capable of being notaries. Today, more than two-thirds of America's notaries are women.

SECTION I - GENERAL BUSINESS CHECKLIST

Now that you have read this section, ask yourself the following questions. Daniel and Judith are available for questions and/or coaching at MakeYourBusinessOurBusiness@gmail.com.

1. Do you have a Business Plan?
2. Do you have a Mission Statement?
3. Do you have an EIN Number?
4. Have you considered what is better—a home office or a business office?
5. If applicable, has your business been registered as a Minority business?
6. Have you secured the necessary business licenses?
7. Have you engaged an accountant and have you decided what your entity should be classified as?
8. Have you chosen a name? Have you made sure it is available with your state?
9. Have you decided on a logo?
10. Have you designed a business card and does it have all of the necessary information?
11. Have you decided on a landline phone vs. wireless?
12. Have you made a protocol for A+Customer Service?
13. Have you decided on a good Invoicing /Accounting system?
14. Have you done your due diligence on accepting credit cards?
15. Are you documenting all Passwords and Serial Numbers?
16. Have you secured a domain name?
17. Have you secured proper insurance?
18. Have you started the website project?

II . HOW TO BECOME
A NOTARY PUBLIC

BELOW ARE SOME OF THE THINGS YOU NEED TO DO TO BECOME A NOTARY AND A NOTARY ENTREPRENEUR! IF YOU HAVE QUESTIONS, PLEASE CONTACT MAKEYOURBUSINESSOURBUSINESS.COM AND DANIEL AND JUDITH WILL BE HAPPY TO ASSIST YOU.

UNDERSTANDING YOUR JOB
AS A NOTARY PUBLIC

There are notaries all over the world. In various countries, notaries have a different job description and are governed differently. Below are a few examples:

FRANCE - THE ROLE OF THE NOTAIRE

https://en.wikipedia.org/wiki/Civil_law_notary

A French *notaire* **is a legal specialist with a public authority mission who draws up authenticated contracts on behalf of his clients. He or she is self-employed.**

NOTARIES IN CHINA

https://en.wikipedia.org/wiki/Public_Notary_Office_of_People%27s_Republic_of_China

The Public Notary Office (Chinese: 公证处 Pinyin:gōng zhèng chù) is a subordinate agency of the Ministry of Justice of the People›s Republic of China. It is responsible for certifying documents according to the Chinese legal system.

NOTARIES IN DENMARK

http://www.forumadvokater.dk/node/276r

If you need a notary in Denmark, you have to contact the city court. Usually, you can visit the notary without a prior appointment. However, the notary's office of the Copenhagen City Court requires an appointment. You do not have to apply at the notary's office/the city court which services the town where you live. Thus, a person living in Roskilde may use the notary's office in Århus. If a person is incapacitated, it is possible to arrange that the notary visits him/her at home or in hospital. In that case, one has to pay the notary's transport expenses.

NOTARIES IN BRAZIL

www.thebrazillawblog.com/important-role-notaries-brazil

Unlike in the United States, for example, a notary in Brazil is a required part of most business transactions. To be accepted, most documents have to first pass by a notary for its stamp of approval. Notaries provide all of the parties involved in a transaction with a layer of safety against fraud. This extra comfort may be desired by the parties or, as if often the case, required by government entities and agencies.

Notaries in Brazil are referred to as *tabeliões*. They are legal professionals who are officially empowered by Brazilian states to perform a variety of notarial activities. The most common notarial activities include those relating to real property transactions, family law, powers of attorney, wills, protesting of bills, recognition of signatures, and authentication of copies of documents.

NOTARIES IN ITALY

www.entering-europe.eu/italy/notary.php

The Italian notary public is the "notaio." Italian notaries also provide legal consultancy regarding contractual obligations. Something different: under the Italian law "legge notarile" (Legge 16 Febbraio 1913 n. 89), they must provide impartial and independent advice to the parties.

NOTARIES IN THE USA

This is critical – In the USA, the job of a notary public is to authenticate that the person is really the person who is signing the document. It is not your job to understand WHY someone is selling a property, or WHY someone needs a Power of Attorney (although understanding those things often helps a great deal); it is your job to authenticate the signature.

There are three important things to keep in mind:

- You need to verify that this is the right person. If you have any doubt, you should not notarize the document. In Indiana, the law used to say if the person swears as to their identity on an affidavit, the notary was permitted to notarize the document. Follow the guidelines set by your governing body.

- The person is not under influence of drugs or alcohol. Obviously, this would impair the signer and he or she may not be signing something they would under other circumstances.

- The person is not being coerced by anyone. If someone looks uncomfortable or it appears that they are being forced or coerced into signing a document, you may say NO.

No notary should notarize a document without valid photo ID and there should be <u>no exceptions</u> to that rule, other than the Critical Witness Rule. (See *Critical Witness Rule*)

Being a notary public is a serious job and you need to protect both your client and yourself.

WATCH FOR SIGNS OF FRAUD!

Many notaries would never knowingly violate notary laws or improperly execute a notarial act. However, the prudent notary should be alert for customers who may try to use you in an intentional attempt to commit fraud. The following are a few items to watch for:

- Altered identification cards: Raised edges around a photo; any visible evidence of tampering. Always verify signatures; observe the birth year to assess the accuracy with the individual before you confirm the address, height, etc.

- Blank spaces on the document; alterations on the document; document not dated, or signature dated after the date of the notarization. Never notarize a signature with correction fluid applied to the document.

- Nervous, aggressive, hostile, or intimidating clients.

- Watch for visible indications of coercion. If one signer is attempting to force or intimidate another signer to sign, do not notarize thedocument.

Some warnings of what to beware of:
www.pawnotary.com
by Joanna Lilly, PAW Notary Service

WHAT DO YOU NEED TO DO
TO BECOME A NOTARY PUBLIC?

The exact qualifications for who can become a notary differ from state to state. You must check with your own state as to the qualifications you are required to have. In general, notary applicants must be 18 years old and a legal resident of the state with no criminal record. Some states require notary applicants to read and write English. Some states also allow residents of neighboring states to become notaries.

While procedures differ from state to state, the general steps to becoming a notary are:

1. Make sure you meet all your state's qualifications. See **LOCAL GOVERNING BODIES OF EACH STATE FOR NOTARY PUBLICS** for links to your own state.

2. Complete and submit an application (be sure to check your state guidelines).

3. Pay the state's filing fee.

4. Get training from an approved education vendor (if applicable). Check your state to see what kind of education is required.

5. Pass a state-administered exam (if applicable).

6. Complete fingerprinting and background check (if applicable).

7. Receive your commission certificate from the state (see example below).

8. Get your surety bond (if applicable). Check your state to see if a bond is required.

9. File your commission paperwork (and bond) with your notary regulating official.

10. Purchase Errors and Omissions Insurance See the Chapter entitled Errors and Omissions Insurance below for more specific information.

11. Buy your notary supplies.

12. **READ THIS BOOK IN ITS ENTIRETY!**

Below is a sample of a Texas Notary Public Commission. Each state is different, but the concept is the same.

IN THE NAME AND BY THE AUTHORITY OF
THE STATE OF TEXAS

Notary Public Commission

TO ALL TO WHOM THESE PRESENTS SHALL COME—GREETINGS:

Whereas **Ima Notary**

has been appointed by the Secretary of State of Texas a Notary Public in the State of Texas. Now, therefore, the above named person is hereby commissioned a Notary Public for the State of Texas under the laws of the State of Texas with all the rights, privileges and emoluments appertaining to said office.

TERM OF OFFICE: 02/25/2011 - 02/25/2015   NOTARY ID# 12345678-9

GREG ABBOTT, GOVERNOR OF TEXAS

ROLANDO B. PABLOS, SECRETARY OF STATE

NOTARY PUBLIC OATH OF OFFICE

State of Texas
County of _____

I, _____, do solemnly swear (or affirm), that I will faithfully execute the duties of the office of notary public of the State of Texas, and will to the best of my ability preserve, protect, and defend the Constitution and laws of the United States and this state, so help me God.

X_____

Sworn to and subscribed before me by on this ____ day of _____, 20____.

Seal   Notary Public Signature

FIND YOURSELF A MENTOR

You have taken the exam, processed your paperwork, you are bonded and insured, and you are ready to notarize. The one other thing you might want to consider is looking for a mentor or a more experienced notary whom you can build a relationship with and ask questions as you encounter different documents. Sometimes it is a quick question and just having someone to ask makes the difference. Sometimes a newer notary isn't sure if he or she should stamp in a certain spot, or where to use the seal. Confidence comes with experience.

You might even want to think about signing a confidentiality agreement and a non-compete agreement with this person, and vice versa, so that if you discover a "niche" for signing, and you share that information, that person cannot jump in front of you and take your idea or your "niche" without your consent.

Why sign Confidentiality and Non-Compete Agreements?

You may discover a company on your street that uses notaries every day. You go and introduce yourself. You give them a price and they agree to use you daily. You share this with your mentor. Your mentor goes the next day and quotes them at a cheaper price and since they are happy to be saving money, you have lost the client. While a Non-Compete is difficult, if not impossible to enforce, its existence may stop this kind of situation.

Since we cannot give legal advice, we cannot provide you with copies of a Confidentiality Agreement or a Non-Compete, but these documents are easy to find on the Internet and we suggest you seriously consider this option.

I have a very unique business, as I am the only notary in my area who offers 24/7 services. I once had a notary come in to help me. She came with a large notebook and, seriously, she was writing down almost every word I said to the point where I became uncomfortable. It was as though she was taking down my business plan and I could see her opening a mirror of my business across the street. I was extremely glad I had asked her to sign a Confidentiality Agreement and a Non-Compete.

ABOUT NOTARY PUBLIC FEES

The fees for all notarial acts are set by the Department of State by regulation. A notary public must not charge or receive a notary public fee in excess of the fees fixed by the Department. The fees of the notary must be separately stated. A notary public may waive the right to charge a fee. If a notary charges fees, the notary must display the fees in a conspicuous place in the notary's place of business or provide fees, upon request, to any person utilizing the services of the notary.

You need to check your state guidelines for further information.

NOTARY FEE COMPARISON THROUGHOUT THE UNITED STATES

For your convenience, attached is a fee comparison chart for notaries throughout the United States.

https://www.nationalnotary.org/knowledge-center/about-notaries/notary-fees-by-state

NOTARY SEALS

Notaries, like yours truly, who like traditional and formal-looking documents, continue to use the notary seal even in states who no longer require it. Many notaries continue to keep embossing seals in their toolboxes because their experience proves that some foreign recipients will reject documents from the U.S. when only an ink-stamp is used. In my experience, sometimes before I have a chance to take the seal out of my bag, a client will ask, "What about the thing, you know, the thing," and they have a sense of relief when they see it. That is because seals have been used for so many years and it is what people are accustomed to seeing.

Inked stamp seals are required in most states. The inked seal provides a crisp impression of a notary's seal and has excellent electronic reproductive capabilities. You can purchase inked seals in both round and rectangular shapes. Be sure to check your specific state guidelines.

Electronic seals are a relatively new concept. Here we focus on seals applied to paper, but you should be aware that electronic seals are growing in popularity and are used with increasing frequency.

APPEARANCES OF SEAL IMPRESSIONS

The standard words that appear on notary seal impressions are (1) the name of the notary owner, (2) his or her commission expiration date, and (3) the words "Notary Public, State of_" surrounding the state's official seal. States individually mandate the type of border that must appear around seal contents.

States also mandate acceptable shapes (round or rectangular) and ranges of size for official notary seals.

CORRECTING SEAL ERRORS

Notary seals must be clear. Reapply the notary seal if the first attempt does not leave a clear impression. Pick another space on the document to reapply the seal; do not attempt to reapply it on top of the flawed impression. It is not necessary to reapply a seal that is inadvertently applied upside down, but one can re-apply it right side up unless state laws dictate otherwise. Some may choose to strike through the flawed impression with a pen.

Seals must be kept in a secure area; never leave a seal unprotected so that it can be used by anyone except its notary owner.

Destroy seals beyond recognition when they are no longer being used.

After a notary leaves his or her position of employment, the notary seal and notary records belong to the notary, even if the employer purchased them. The seal and records must remain in the possession of the notary.

If an employer does not understand, please refer him or her to your state's laws or to your notary public administrator for more information.

NOTARY SEAL REQUIREMENTS FOR U.S. STATES AND TERRITORIES

Section 405.019 of the Texas Government Code requires the secretary of state to compile an annual list of those U.S. states and territories that require notaries public to validate certificates of acknowledgment, proofs of written instruments or jurats by attaching an official seal. The secretary has provided both a chart summarizing which states and territories require such a seal and a more detailed list referencing the authority under which the seal is required, and when available, the specifications for the seal.

State	Seal Required?
Alabama	Y
Alaska	Y
American Samoa	Y
Arizona	Y
Arkansas	Y
California	Y
Colorado	Y
Connecticut	N
Delaware	Y
District of Columbia	Y
Florida	Y
Georgia	Y
Guam	Y
Hawaii	Y
Idaho	Y
Illinois	Y
Indiana	Y
Iowa	Y
Kansas	Y
Kentucky	N
Louisiana	N
Maine	N
Maryland	Y
Massachusetts	Y
Michigan	N
Minnesota	Y
Mississippi	Y
Missouri	Y

State	Seal Required?
Montana	Y
Nebraska	Y
Nevada	Y
New Hampshire	Y
New Jersey	N
New Mexico	Y
New York	N
North Carolina	Y
North Dakota	Y
North Marianas	Y
Ohio	Y
Oklahoma	Y
Oregon	Y
Pennsylvania	Y
Puerto Rico	Y
Rhode Island	N
South Carolina	Y
South Dakota	Y
Tennessee	Y
Texas	Y
Utah	Y
Vermont	N
Virgin Islands	Y
Virginia	Y
Washington	Y
West Virginia	Y
Wisconsin	Y
Wyoming	Y

NOTARY STAMPS

Self-inking stamps are the most popular and the easiest to use. Two things important to keep in mind:

When making an impression, it must be made so that it is neat and clear and will be accepted by the recipient;

The stamp must not obscure the notary's signature or any of the text on the document.

Some notaries carry more than one stamp which alleviates the problem of a stamp suddenly running out of ink or, more importantly, if you run into a document with so little space that you cannot use a stamp. That might be the time to use an acknowledgment or a jurat. Place on line through the editing notary certificate, initial near the line, and write the words "see attached". Then you may complete, sign and stamp the certificate and make sure it is stapled to the document.

To order stamps, please click on MakeYourBusinessOurBusiness.com.

NOTARY JOURNALS

Recordkeeping is an essential part of any business and for the most part, the most annoying task. I always say that when I am ultra-successful I will continue to run my business exactly the way I do it today, but I will hire a full-time bookkeeper.

A notary journal is an essential part of your business and you have to do it; skipping it is not an option. Keeping a notary journal or record book has been a part of the process for as long as there have been notaries in America. Below you will see a State-by-State chart of where Notary Journals are required. You should also check with your own state as to their guidelines.

There is a chapter in this book called "If You Did Not Write It, You Did Not Say It," and that also applies to a notary journal. You know what you did, for whom, and what you were paid, and that is of importance if you are ever called to court and need to bring a copy of the record. Good records of properly performed notarizations are evidence that you as the notary have taken all proper steps to follow the best practices of your commission.

Be advised that case law has often supported the need for notary journals and at times may be considered prima facie evidence of the facts stated within it.

You will want to include in your Journal:

1. The date and time of notarization;
2. The name of the document(s)
3. The name and address of each person signing the document(ss) or who serves as a witness;
4. Identification of all signers; and
5. The fee charged for each notarial act.

In Pennsylvania, the new rules (Rulona) effective October 26, 2017 state that if you want to use an electronic journal, it will need to be "tamper-proof." What that means is that once the entry is saved you cannot go back and make any changes. I am using NotaryAct. I find it easy to learn and it fits all the requirements of the State of Pennsylvania.

This is a quote from the Rulona Rules: "A journal may be created on a tangible medium (paper) or in an electronic format. A notary public may maintain a separate journal for tangible records and for electronic records. If the journal is maintained on a tangible medium, it must be a bound register with numbered pages. If the journal is maintained in an electronic format, it must be in a **tamper-evident electronic format** complying with the regulations of the department."

Remember that a notary faces unlimited liability for any errors or omissions he/she makes in the performance of a notarial act. Just one claim of an incomplete or improper notarial act against the notary can cause catastrophic financial damage. Your record book entries can help you reconstruct your notarial acts if you are ever called into court. If your state's notary laws do not address every detail of performing a notarial act, the record book can show that you followed the dictates of good notarial procedure.

ELECTRONIC NOTARY JOURNALS

A notary's journal exists to function as a record of a notary's activities. It verifies that a notary notarized the signature of a person on a certain document on a certain date. Paper journals do a great job of capturing basic information about a notarial act. However, there have been some advancements that now allow notaries in most States to capture notarial acts in an electronic journal. For example, NotaryAct saves me significant time when I am recording information about my signings. The scan feature automatically enters names and addresses of signers, crucial details about the identification they provided, and captures the GPS time, date and location of the signing.

Before you switch to an electronic journal you should consult with the Secretary of State office in your state or with one of the reputable Notary Associations to make sure it is acceptable in your particular state.

I have made the transition to an electronic journal. After doing much research, I chose NotaryAct. NotaryAct has been developed by legal counsel. Because of this, I felt the most confident that I am entering my information in accordance with the laws of the State of Pennsylvania. I have found that it is an easier process and I can use either my smartphone or my iPad. On the next page, you will see an image of what a journal page looks like.

Make Your Business Our Business

New Entry

Judith
Lawrence
account active

New Entry

Current Enterprise: Individual

SIGNER

Search

New Entry

Journal

Reports

My Account

Settings

Logout

First Name:
Middle Initial:
Last Name:
Address:
  Zip Code
  State
  City
  Address
Email:
ID Type:
ID Gov't Issuing Agency:
ID Issued Date:
ID Expiration Date:
ID Picture: Choose File No file chosen

Signature:

✕

NOTARIAL ACT

Date: 03/08/2018 16:55:46
Location:
  Zip Code
  State
  City
  Address
Type:
Fee:

1/2

91

STATE BY STATE NOTARY
JOURNAL REQUIREMENTS

This chart will be extremely helpful in determining your state's journal requirements:

Notary Journal Requirements per State

Key:

■ Notary record book **not** required.

■ Notary Journal required.

■ Not required for standard notarial acts, but required for other acts.

□ Not required for paper notarial acts, required for electronic.

Courtesy of Notary Journal Underwriters Inc.

Though a state may not require a notary to use a notary journal or record book, we recommend that every notary use one. As mentioned before, a notary journal helps you stay organized and serves as a record of your notarial acts. This is extremely important and can help you if you're ever accused of falsifying a record or completing a notarial act incorrectly. In situations like that, the notary journal can act as a support to your defense. All record books should be kept in a secure location. As with the notary seal and notary commission, your record book contains sensitive information that should not be readily available to others. We recommend keeping your seal and record book in a locked drawer in your desk while at work or at home. Never leave your record book on your desk unattended.

Though a state may not require a notary to use a notary journal or record book, we recommend every notary use one. A notary journal helps you stay organized and serves as a record of your notarial acts. This is extremely important and can help you if you're ever accused of falsifying a record or completing a notarial act incorrectly. In situations like that, the notary journal can act as a support to your defense. All record books should be kept in a secure location. As with the notary seal and notary commission, your record book contains sensitive information that should not be readily available to others. We recommend keeping your seal and record book in a locked drawer in your desk while at work or at home. Never leave your record book on your desk unattended.

Alabama: Not required. Alaska: Not Required. Arkansas: Not required.

Arizona: Required. A notary is only allowed to keep one record book at a time, unless some entries are confidential. If you have confidential and non-confidential records, you are allowed two notary record books.

California: Required. A notary is only allowed to keep one record book at a time. It should be in chronological order and should be stored in a secure location. The California Notary Handbook contains what needs to be included in a record book entry.

Colorado: Required. Connecticut: Not required.

Delaware: Not required for paper notarial acts, but it is required for electronic notarial acts. Title 29, 4314 contains the law requiring a notary journal for an electronic notarization and the required information.

District of Columbia: Required. Florida: Required for online notarizations. Not required for any other notarizations.

Georgia: Not required.

Hawaii: Required. The record book must be soft covered, contain numbered pages, and should not exceed 11" high and 16.5" wide when open. Section 456-15 defines what information should be included in each entry.

Idaho: Not required. Illinois: Not required. Indiana: Not required. Iowa: Not required.

Kansas: Not required.

Kentucky: Kentucky - Required for electronic (online) notarizations only

Louisiana: Not required.

Maine: Not required. It is only required that Maine notaries keep a record of all marriage ceremonies they officiate. If you decide to keep a record book in Maine, it is unlawful to use the thumbprint of a signer in your records.

Maryland: Required.

Massachusetts: Required. You can only have one active record book at a time. It is the property of the notary, even if your company paid for your commission. It is required that you keep your record book for seven years after your commission expires.

Michigan: Required only for remote electronic notarial acts.

Minnesota: Not required.

Mississippi: Required. It is required to have only one active record book and the record book should be permanently bound with numbered pages.

Missouri: Required. The record book must be permanently bound and have numbered pages.

Montana: Required. In your notary Handbook, it specifies the required information to be included with each entry.

Nevada: Required. The record book is required to be bound and have numbered pages. It should also be stored in a secure location, such as a locked drawer.

New Hampshire: Not required. New Jersey: Not required.

New Mexico: Not required. New York: Not required.

North Carolina: Not required.

North Dakota: Not required.

Ohio: Required for online notarizations only.

Oklahoma: Required for absentee ballots; required for remote online notarizations

Oregon: Required.

Pennsylvania: Required. All notarial acts must be recorded (electronic and paper), and the notary is only allowed to have one active record book at a time.

Rhode Island: Not required. South Carolina: Not required. South Dakota: Not required.

Tennessee: Required if the Notary or Notary's employer charges a fee.

Texas: Required. All notarial acts (paper and electronic) must be recorded. There are also laws about your employer seeing information in your record book, and how to handle a lost or stolen record book.

U.S. Virgin Islands: Required.

Utah: Required for remote notarizations. Not required for all other notarial acts.

Vermont: Not required.

Virginia: Required. A record book is required only for electronic notarial acts. No record for paper notarial acts is required. If the electronic act is completed via video, the notary is required to record the notarial act and store a copy. The Virginia Notary Handbook in section 47.1-14 explains the requirement for electronic notaries.

Washington: Required.

West Virginia: Not required but permitted for electronic notarial acts. Wisconsin: Not required.

Wyoming: Not required.

CONFIDENTIALITY

In some instances, "confidentiality" refers to not discussing internal goings-on with co-workers. In other instances, it refers to not sharing trade secrets and other company information with competitors, the press, or anyone outside of your company. In every instance, respect for confidentiality is essential to the success of your business. Below is an instance of a lack of confidentiality:

> Alice is not well, and she has not yet told anyone about her condition. She comes to the notary to get a Will and a Power of Attorney signed. It so happens that she and the notary knew each other in high school years ago and they had a nice chat. Alice tells the notary about her illness.

> That evening, the notary met another old friend (Jane) for dinner. While they were going down in the elevator, the notary told Jane about their mutual friend, Alice, and her illness. What the notary did not know is that Jane's mother and Alice's mother are still very close friends and see each other often. Jane tells her mother about poor Alice and her mother calls her friend to express how sorry she is about Alice.

In case you think this is unusual, it is not. These things happen on a regular basis.

I make it a practice not to bring what I have heard in the office out of the office, especially in an elevator or in a restaurant. I might recount a story, but I do not mention a name.

Documents are very important to the people who are signing them. They come to a commissioned officer to get a notary done and we need to make sure that the trust they place in us is not abused in any way.

A NOTARY MUST **NEVER** GIVE LEGAL ADVICE

A notary must be careful never to give legal advice. Notaries have lost their commissions because later a client says, "That's what the notary told me to do." Remember, as a notary you are authenticating a signature, not what is contained in the document. Also remember that if someone looks uncomfortable or looks like he or she is being forced to sign the document, you as a notary have the right to abstain from notarizing the document(s).

You always need to be careful, but you need to be especially careful with mortgages and deeds and other recordable documents.

Let's make up a scenario.

> Ted comes to the office and asks, "Should I sign this Power of Attorney? My mom is in the hospital and I need to take care of everything." Jill, the notary says, "Well, Ted, it looks good to me, let's do it. Ted signs the document, Jill notarizes it, it is properly witnessed, and Ted leaves. But it was a Financial Power of Attorney and not a Power of Attorney allowing Ted to make medical decisions on behalf of his mother. Ted puts the document away. Two weeks later his mother takes a turn for the worse, she can no longer speak for herself and needs immediate surgery. Ted is surely glad he got that Power of Attorney signed but it was incorrect because he was not authorized to make medical decisions for his mother. His mother dies and Ted sues the notary because she said, "it looks good to me" and that was incorrect for Ted's situation. It could have been avoided if Jill had said, "Ted, I think you should consult someone to make sure this document covers all of your needs. If you do not have the name of an attorney, I could suggest someone. As a notary, I cannot offer you my opinion as to whether this is the right document for you and your mother."

So, (this is confession time) I once bent the rules. . .

A beautiful elderly woman showed up in my notary office at 6:30 P.M., her basket in tow. She had walked 18 blocks to get to my office and she was 94 years old. She sat down and said, "Hon, I really need a will. And you have to hurry up because I have to go home." I thought she meant she was late for dinner, but I was wrong. I said, "Where is home?" and she said, "Home, hon. I'm too old to stay here too much longer."

So first I tried the "call a lawyer" suggestion and she agreed. She made an appointment and after meeting with the lawyer she came back to my office and said he did not understand.

My next suggestion was that she go to a specific store where they sell templates. I thought that would be helpful. Now remember, at 94, she was looking for a basic will, not eight pages, the kind that all of our grandparents signed—I leave this to this person, and that to that person. She did as I asked, but the template did not help her.

Instinctively I knew what she wanted, and so, that night, I recalled the hundreds of wills I had typed as a legal secretary. I drafted a plain will that said she was leaving everything (all $1,234.00) to her granddaughters. It was a page and a half. When she saw it, her face lit up and she could not thank me enough. Signed, sealed, and notarized.

I could not take any payment from her because she did not have anything, but she offered to go to church and pray for me and I gladly accepted her offer.

I don't recommend you break the rules, but sometimes it's okay, and she will be forever in my heart.

A quote from the NNA:

"Many signers will ask you for advice or assistance regarding their document. Unless you are an attorney, you should always say no because it would be the <u>unauthorized practice of law</u>*, and you could be held liable."*

PROFESSIONALISM

Think about this…a person comes to your home and they look like they just got out of bed. They are quite adept at what they do, the job gets done, but they leave no impression.

Then think about the person who walks in and looks professional, not necessarily in a suit and tie, but crisp and sharp. That person does the same job with the same skill but at the end of the signing, you ask for a business card, and you perhaps inquire as to what other notarial services that person may have to offer. I have found myself in the homes of athletes and politicians. You never know where opportunity lies.

It is very important to look and act as professional as possible. A couple of rules:

- Always be well-groomed and neat and clean; no jeans and no sneakers;

- Turn down the ringer on your cell phone before the closing. It is distracting and sometimes it is hard enough to keep the attention of the people who are signing;

- If offered alcohol (lots of people are sharing a glass of wine when you arrive and ask if you would like a glass), decline. The last thing you need is an error in the closing documents and to have the signers say, "Well, maybe we shouldn't have offered that notary a glass of wine";

- Don't discuss business, religion, politics or any other controversial subject.

- And this is the hardest one … you will need to gauge your audience to determine if you should engage them in any conversation other than about the closing. I have done thousands of closings. Sometimes the people are friendly and want to know a little about you, which is fine, but sometimes they are not interested in small talk and just want to sign the papers and get you out of there. My rule is to let the client be your guide. Sometimes, after it is all done, I feel comfortable giving my business a little commercial plug and leave a card, but sometimes I pack my bag, shake their hand(s) and leave.

- If your signing is taking place in a hospital or a nursing home, try to get it done as quickly as possible without sacrificing accuracy; and

- Lastly, NEVER discuss your fee for the service you are providing except with the person who is paying your fee. If it is a closing for a title company, and the borrower asks about your fee, just say you are not authorized to release that information.

There is also digital professionalism, which we will discuss in our chapter entitled Social Media.

KNOW HOW TO ESTABLISH YOURSELF AS AN EXPERT

A notary must always follow the rules of the particular state in which he or she is commissioned. However, most successful notaries find a way to make people feel that they are the expert at what they do.

I know notaries who go to a signing with a book of rules and put it out on the table.

I personally bring a selection of blue pens. In the right environment, I call them my "magic blue pens." I explain the reasoning for signing with blue ink; that the documents will be photocopied, scanned, or faxed and if someone ever wants to seek out the original document that he or she signed, remember that the notary had you sign all of the documents in blue ink. That establishes me as the expert.

Find your own way, whether it is blue pens or whatever is most comfortable for you, but I can guarantee that once you establish yourself as an expert, your client(s) will tend to be more cooperative and your signing will almost always head to a smooth completion.

ACCEPTING
PROPER IDENTIFICATION

Anyone who is signing a document (including witnesses) will need to present a valid piece of photo ID. There can be a few exceptions to this rule; please follow your local state guidelines.

In Pennsylvania, for example, passports ARE acceptable identification EXCEPT if it is a PennDOT transaction; they do not accept passports as identification.

If the signing is for someone who is ill, the notary should make sure in advance someone will have his or her identification available.

Some states, such as California, Florida and Tennessee, provide specific lists of acceptable IDs. In these states, if the ID is not on the list, it is not acceptable. If you live in one of these states, you may rely on the list but check your local state guidelines to be sure.

A number of states, such as Illinois, Colorado, and Pennsylvania, prescribe specific elements for information an acceptable ID must-have. Notaries in these states must exercise some judgment in determining whether to accept an ID as presented.

Finally, a number of states, such as Kansas, Minnesota and New York, have laws that offer little to no guidance about available IDs. The NNA recommends that these notaries follow the guidelines delineated in the Notary Public Code of Professional Responsibility. (See link under Best Practices).

Here is a great article about what can happen when you don't pay attention to proper identification:

October 12, 2017, 123 Notary
A Notary Gets Sued Because of Scrambled ID
http://blog.123notary.com/?p=19443

MAKING CHANGES TO A DOCUMENT ... OR NOT

A notary must never change a document. I have seen very little exception to this rule. However, there are times when a change may need to be made. One example is if a middle initial is wrong. If everything else on the document is correct, I sometimes ask the client to cross out the middle initial, write the correct one, and then initial that he or she made this correction. It is very important to note that even this will not be acceptable on a mortgage, a deed, or any other document which will be filed of record.

When I am notarizing something that could be important in years to come (i.e., estate planning documents, a prenup, a lease), I often suggest to a client that he or she initial each page of the document in the lower right-hand corner. I explain that this means that if someone were to attempt to change a page, they could not do so because the page is initialed. (See *Know How to Establish Yourself as the Expert*)

SHOULD YOU NOTARIZE A DOCUMENT THAT HAS ALREADY BEEN SIGNED?

Have you ever been presented with a document that has already been signed? Based upon your state guidelines, you may have two options:

1. Acknowledgment. This document is a signed declaration that the document has been executed freely and voluntarily. The signer is basically only acknowledging his or her signature, not the date or time of the signing. As long as the signer is present before the notary, the notary may proceed to notarize. As a notary, your certificate of acknowledgment should always state the date the person appeared before you. When you list this in your journal, you should list both the date of the document and the date the signer appeared before you.

2. Oath. An oath or affirmation requires that the signer appears before the notary, he or she must swear or affirm as to the truthfulness of the statements made in the document and sign the document in your presence. If the document has already been signed, he or she can sign his or her name again, above or next to the first time it was signed. The notary may then proceed to notarize. You may want to record this procedure in your journal.

JOINING ORGANIZATIONS

The following is a list of organizations in which I maintain memberships on behalf of my company. It can be costly to do this, so you need to put your dollars where they will give the most exposure and/or business. There are several other wonderful organizations which I would like to join and, conversely, there are some organizations which I joined and did not re-join because they did not work for me. Study them carefully.

I will give you two examples.

I am an auto tags agent and the Pennsylvania Association of Notaries has been irreplaceable to me as far as my auto tags business. I got my license through them and their help desk is responsive and an invaluable source of information.

The second example is the Philadelphia Area Concierge Association. I am city- based and do a fair amount of work for hotels. I have met many concierges through this organization and have presented at their meetings several times.

So again, look at your vision and what you want to do with your business and then pick a few organizations that will help you.

Some local examples of my memberships:

- National Notary Association
- American Association of Notaries
- Indiana Notary Association
- Pennsylvania Association of Notaries
- Philadelphia Area Concierge Association
- National Association of Professional Women
- National Association of Women Business Owner's
- Pennsylvania Board of Elections
- Citizens for Diplomacy
- Center City Residents Association

JOINING NOTARY WEBSITES

You will find an abundance of notary websites. If you take the next step and become a Certified Signing Agent, you will need to register with many signing companies in order to get work. Each of those companies have a website and you will have to register with them before they will give you work.

But right now, you are a notary and you are looking for assignments.

One of the sites I like is **123 Notary**. There is no question about the legitimacy of the notaries. The site provides updated articles on notary policies and procedures. There is a cost to become a member of 123 Notary but it is well worth the dollars you will spend.

I also recommend **Notary Rotary**. It has many of the same characteristics as 123 and I personally have received some good assignments from this site. There is also a fee to become a member and also well worth it

My third recommendation is **Notary Café**. Notary's Café's database is used by many professional notary signing companies. It is easy to use and has been around for a long time; I have gotten some good work from this site.

Signingagent.com is a notary database that is excellent to receive general notary work because it allows you to place a profile along with a photo of yourself.

People can search these sites by name, by city, by zip code, and by credentials. If you decide to join these sites, it is important that you spend time on your profile and the notes sections. You will be asked a series of questions and it is important that you answer them all. Tell them if you offer 24/7 services, if you accept assignments via email, if you include Apostilles on your array of services, etc.; give the search engine a way to find you if a new client is looking for someone exactly like you.

Don't waste words. For example:

DO NOT SAY, "I became a notary about 10 years ago and have been accepting assignments since that time."

SAY: "Practicing Notary for 10 Years. Have handled estate documents, mortgage closings, and refinance transactions." Keep it clear and concise and make sure you give the prospective reader the ability to quickly understand that you are experienced and exactly what you have done.

WHAT IS REMOTE NOTARIZATION?

The name "remote notary" is derived from the fact that the notary serves a non-local customer directly over the internet.

A remote notary is a legally commissioned notary public who is authorized to conduct notarizations over the internet via digital tools and a live audio/video call.

All notaries, no matter how they perform their services, must watch as someone signs a document. Historically, this has required that the notary and signer must travel to meet one another in person where the notary acts as a witness during the signing event.

Because remote notaries conduct their notarizations online, they have the benefit of digital tools to assist them during the process. Under Virginia law, people conducting remote notarizations are held to a much higher ID verification standard. Today, for typical notarizations, nearly half of all states require no ID at all or permit an expired ID.

Remote notaries have digital tools to assist them. For example, remote notarizations require that a customer answer identity challenge questions, typically called **Knowledge Based Authentication**, before they may sign a document. This ensures that the customer is who they claim to be. Also, because it is conducted online, a remote notarization can be recorded – allowing anyone to verify the transaction after the fact.

These are only a few examples of how technology is able to assist remote notaries:

KNOWLEDGE BASED AUTHENTICATION

Knowledge-Based Authentication is an identity authentication method that asks questions based on detailed information an individual knows. This information is usually more advanced than the kind of information a fraudster might be able to access through your email or computer. Knowledge-Based Authentication is often used along with another type of authentication (such as a password) to increase security. There are two kinds of Knowledge-Based Authentication — static and dynamic.

STATIC KNOWLEDGE-BASED AUTHENTICATION

If you've ever needed to reset a password, you've probably encountered static knowledge-based authentication. With this method, you pick security questions and give answers that are stored and referenced later. The user controls the questions and answers with this type of knowledge-based authentication.

Static KBA, also referred to as "shared secrets" or "shared secret questions", is commonly used by banks, financial services companies, and e-mail providers to prove the identity of the customer before allowing account access, or as a fallback if the user forgets their password. At the point of initial contact with a customer, a business using static KBA must collect the information to be shared between the provider and customer, most commonly the question(s) and corresponding answer(s). This data must then be stored, only to be retrieved when the customer comes back to access the account.

DYNAMIC KNOWLEDGE-BASED AUTHENTICATION

Dynamic Knowledge-Based Authentication takes authentication to the next level by generating questions that only apply to one specific person. This type of Knowledge-Based Authentication does not require any previous relationship with the customer, so it is an attractive option for e-signature users that need to be authenticated instantly. We sometimes call these questions "out-of-wallet" questions because the information couldn't be found in a person's wallet if it was stolen. The questions are generated from the user's credit history or public records.

Many regulatory bodies, including the IRS, require that e-signature users be authenticated using dynamic Knowledge Based Authentication.

STATES THAT ENACTED LAWS

It all started in 2011 when the state of Virginia introduced the Electronic Notaries Act. This law made e-notarizations and remote, or online, notarizations possible by enabling signers from anywhere in the world to appear live before a commissioned notary public on a screen via Skype, Facetime, or another audio-video teleconference option and get a document notarized.

- Montana became the second state to legalize online notarization in 2015. Signers must be residents of Montana and the transaction must meet specific criteria laid out in the law, which includes that the signer must be known personally to the notary or verified by a credible witness.

- <u>Florida</u> authorized webcam notarizations in 2015. However, the practice is limited to certain law enforcement and correctional officers who are permitted to administer oaths and affirmations.

- <u>Nebraska</u> passed a law to legalize remote electronic notarization and provide standards for the use of video and audio conference technology to complete notarial acts. The law is effective July 1, 2017.

- <u>Kentucky</u> and <u>Minnesota</u> are set to enact the <u>Revised Uniform Law on Notarial Acts (RULONA)</u> to be effective on June 29 and Aug. 1, 2017, respectively, which will allow a notary to perform a notarial act using audio-video technology for a signer outside the U.S. <u>Washington</u> is also proposing a bill to adopt RULONA.

- <u>Maryland</u>, <u>Oklahoma</u>, and <u>Texas</u> are each considering bills that will authorize notaries to perform electronic and online notarizations. They should go into effect Oct. 1, 2017, Nov. 1, 2017 and Jan. 1, 2018, respectively. Pennsylvania has also introduced an online notarization bill.

- <u>Washington, D.C.</u> introduced a bill March 7, 2017 that clarifies electronic notarizations, outlines how audio-video recordings can be used, and define authentication for electronic signatures. It is currently in a congressional review period.

- <u>Louisiana</u>'s legislature requested that the Louisiana State Law Institute look into electronic notarizations and remote e-notarizations. The Institute's report and recommendations were provided in February 2017, and they are expected to determine the future of e-notarizations.

COMPANIES THAT OFFER THE SERVICE

Five companies are presently providing service using web-based proprietary systems:

DocVerify, Irvine, California

Notarize, Alexandria, Virginia *(service through mobile app) NotaryCam, Alexandria, Virginia

Safedocs, Alamo, California Signix, Chattanooga, Tennessee

ELECTRONIC SIGNATURES

Any time you make a purchase with a credit card and are asked to sign a digital pad or type your PIN to get money out of your bank's ATM machine, you are using an electronic signature or eSignature. Anytime you make a purchase on the internet and click the "submit order" button, you are electronically signing a purchase agreement. Electronic signatures have become commonplace in the retail world, and they are also becoming commonplace in larger transactions, such as making an offer on a home purchase. eSignatures can be made in a number of different ways but they are considered as legally valid as a signature on a paper document (often called a "wet" signature).

ELECTRONIC NOTARIZATION

Electronic notarization, or eNotarization, is essentially the same as a paper notarization except the document being notarized is in a digital form and the notary signs with an electronic signature. Depending upon state law, the information in the notary's seal may be placed on the electronic document as a graphic image or other available means. But all other elements of a traditional, paper notarization remain, <u>including the requirement for the signer to physically appear before the notary</u>.

WEBCAM NOTARIZATION

People often confuse eNotarization with webcam notarization, believing that they are the same, which is not so. Webcam notarization utilizes video and audio technology on the internet to allow signers to personally appear before and communicate with the notary at the time of notarization. With traditional signings, the signer is in the notary's physical presence.

To date, only six states have enacted laws permitting the use of webcam technology for notarial acts. In 2011, Virginia became the first state. Montana and Florida joined in 2015. Both states limit the circumstances under which webcam notarization can be performed. Texas, Nevada and Ohio have also passed laws authorizing online notarizations.

A number of states, including California, New Jersey, Oklahoma, Oregon, Rhode Island, and Wisconsin have issued public statements that notarizations using online communication are prohibited and signers are still required to physically appear before notaries.

E-CLOSING

An E-closing, or electronic closing, is a mortgage closing in which all documents remain in digital form. They are signed, notarized and returned to the title company or lender in digital form, and nothing is printed out. An E-closing can be conducted with the borrowers and notary in each other's physical presence or online using video-audio technology.

ONLINE CLOSING

An online closing is an electronic closing that is conducted online without the borrower and notary being in each other's physical presence. The personal appearance requirement for the notarization is satisfied via the internet using webcam technology.

ICLOSE

iClose is a web-based closing system offered by one settlement services provider. With this system, the borrower physically appears before a notary to sign a Limited Power of Attorney (LPOA) in paper form. The LPOA allows a representative of the title company or lender to sign the borrower's mortgage documents. Typically, the borrower will then log onto the iClose system to review and approve the loan document using an electronic signature. The title company or lender representative signs all paper documents in the closing package, including the mortgage or deed of trust and a title company or lender notary notarizes the representative's signature.

SECTION II - HOW TO BECOME A NOTARY PUBLIC

Now that you have read this section, ask yourself the following questions. Daniel and Judith are available for questions and/or coaching at MakeYourBusinessOurBusiness@gmail.com.

1. Have you taken all steps required in your specific state to become a notary?

2. Have you made sure you have the correct insurance required by your state?

3. Have you studied best practices in your specific state?

4. Have you researched the requirements for a notary seal?

5. Have you researched the requirements for a notary stamp?

6. Have you researched the notary journal requirements in your specific state?

7. Have you secured property notary identification?

8. Do you have all necessary forms and supplies?

III. LET'S TALK TECHNOLOGY EQUIPMENT NEEDED TO START YOUR BUSINESS

WIFI CONNECTION

You will need a WiFi connection. In the early days of the Internet, people would sit down at their desktop computer, log on to the Internet (usually via dial-up), surf for a period of time, and then log off and continue on with the rest of their life. This logging-on and logging-off is now a thing of the past. Today, people are connected to the Internet at all times and from anywhere, and it is primarily the smartphone that is responsible for this ubiquitous connectivity. If you have an office, you will need WiFi both at home and in the office.

COMPUTERS

Buying a computer is one of your most important tasks. Below is a spec sheet which I asked my colleagues at Provident Technology to suggest for our readers. But there are so many considerations: what you feel you will be doing in your business, will you be doing mostly documents, spreadsheets, graphics, or perhaps even videos?

- **Recommended PC Specs: Manufacturer**: Dell, Lenovo, or HP
  Processor: Intel Core i5 processor or better
  Memory: Minimum of 8gb of RAM
  Hard Disk: Either a Solid State Drive (SSD) at 200gb or more for best speed performance, or a regular Hard Drive at 500gb minimum (provided that it is a 7200 RPM instead of a 5400 RPM disc).
  Operating System: Windows 10 Professional
  Network: Built-in Ethernet recommended, but Wi-Fi will suffice.

I recommend consulting with a tech professional before upgrading or purchasing a computer. As to whether you should purchase a laptop or a desktop, that is completely a personal choice and depends on how you run your business. For me, I like a large desktop (I have a 24" all-in-one) at the office and a laptop at home.

You also might want to consider a tablet for purposes of flexibility. If you need "on the spot" reporting, it is the way to go.

LASER PRINTERS

Especially if you are planning to become a Certified Signing Agent, your printer is the most important purchase you will make. Title companies and signing companies have a lot in common; they often produce documents at the very last minute. You will need a high-speed laser printer that can push out the documents quickly. A two-tray printer is necessary, as often they sneak in a few legal-size documents. You will need color capability. If you are considering an Ink Jet, you might rethink, because if the paper gets wet, the ink will smudge all over the paper and make the documentinvalid.

Many companies now say, "Send me a quick scan and I'll get right back to you." Your scanner needs to have legal, letter, and color capability.

Recommended Laser Printer Specs:

Provident Technology recommends Brother printers for small office environments. Brother printers combine affordability with a proven track record of providing small business environments with reliable tech support and quality printing. Perhaps more important than your choice in brand, we strongly recommend printers with an available Ethernet connection rather than Wi-Fi. Wi-Fi-only printers often experience intermittent communications issues with computers on the network and thus are not recommended for heavy-duty, business-level use.

WARNING: BE SURE BOTH YOUR PRINTER AND SCANNER ACCEPT BOTH LEGAL AND LETTER SIZE PAPERS ... YOU WILL USE THERE FEATURES CONSTANTLY.

FAX MACHINES

I have chosen not to have a fax machine; I use www.myfax.com. I scan the document and then fax it through my computer. Faxing is so infrequent these days (it seems everyone would rather have a scan e-mailed to them) so this is my way of saving the cost of another line and those monthly fees.

Of course, there are all kinds of combination printers. I have a printer/ scanner/fax combination which I like a lot, but it took a few printer purchases before I found the right one for my printing needs.

WHY AND HOW TO USE OUTLOOK

In my personal opinion, for your business to be successful, you need to use Microsoft Outlook as your email provider.

This is very important because so many people use Outlook it and will send you invites that will appear on your calendar. Plus, it will keep you organized and efficient. And for Gmail users, the good news is that Outlook and Gmail can now be integrated.

Here are the different functions of Outlook:

IN-BOX

I do not handle my email like this (I prefer to answer them as I receive them), but Outlook provides you with a Five Folder System of answering your mail:

1. Inbox: the inbox is a holding pen. Emails shouldn't stay here any longer than it takes for you to file them into another folder. The exception to this rule is when you respond immediately and are waiting for an immediate response.

2. Today: Everything that requires a response today.

3. This Week: Everything that requires a response before the end of the week.

4. This Month/Quarter: Everything that needs a longer-term response. Depending on your role, you many need a monthly folder. Others can operate on a quarterly basis.

5. FYI: Many items I receive are informational. If I think I may need to reference an email again, I'll save it to this folder.

FOLDERS

Whether you use Outlook or any other type of digital folder system, you need to get into the habit from day one of creating folders for anything

(i) that you may want or need to use again in the future, and (ii) anything that you don't want to lose if and when the system purges older files or documents. This reduces clutter in your inbox.

To create a folder on your desktop, right-click on your mouse, select NEW FOLDER, and the CREATE A NEW FOLDER dialogue box will appear. Here you can name the folder and select where you would like it to be located. You can organize your folders in a way that makes the most sense for the way you work.

For example, you can create a folder for your EIN number, your notary commission, a background check, a CNSA Certificate, and/or your tax information. By creating these folders and labeling them correctly, you will always be able to go to that folder and quickly get the information you need. It saves the "I know I had it but I will have to look for it and then I'll get back to you" situation.

Once your folders are set up, you should be able to access them on your phones and on your tablets. This means <u>instant access</u> to important information when you are at a meeting or at a conference or with a client. Perhaps you are at the bank and all they need is that EIN Number and there it is, right on your phone in a folder called "EIN." Or perhaps you are at a signing and they ask for your commission number and there it is, right on your phone. The list goes on, but you get the point.

You can drag and drop emails into folders but be careful – sometimes the items will accidentally drop somewhere other than the intended location and emails and folders are misplaced.

CONTACTS

Your contacts are of utmost importance for a myriad of reasons. Running a business is fast-paced and you will need to keep up. Today, when most business people receive a call, they immediately save the number to contacts. Sometimes people save the information by name; sometimes it is smarter to save the information by the company.

A good example of this is that I speak to Secretaries of States regarding Apostilles across the country. I save everything under Apostille CA (Apostille California); Apostille NY (New York), etc. If there is a specific name of a person, I include that in my notes. This keeps me very efficient; I only have to Google one time when I am first looking for the information and after that, I have what I need.

CALENDAR

I have become addicted to the calendar system in Outlook. Not only does it maintain my appointments, it reminds me of them prior to the appointment, I know what time I have to be there and where I have to be. You can set it up so it reminds you of people's birthdays and other occasions such as dates when bills are due to be paid. Some people still like to use a manual appointment book; if you are one of them, I suggest you do both.

HOW TO WORK FROM
A REMOTE LOCATION

The best way to work from a remote location (away from your main computer) is to use www.gotomypc.com.

Here is how it works: You sign up for an account and receive a username, a password, and an access code. You log in, follow the prompts, and you will be viewing your desktop. You will have access to everything that is on your main frame computer. This will not work unless you leave the mainframe computer on – it has to have something to connect to. I find this to be extremely efficient.

HOW TO USE GOOGLE DRIVE

Google Drive allows you to store documents on your Google drive and in some instances, share the drive with someone else.

In order to use your Google Drive, you have to have a Gmail account. The account provides you with a drive. When you save your documents, you save them right on the drive. So anyone who has access to your Google Account will be able to have access to your documents.

If you are working on a special project, you may not want to use the same Google drive where you keep all your working documents, so you can create a specific Gmail account for that specific project and you will be able to share the documents with all of your collaborators for that project.

It is really quite simple:

1. Create a Gmail account – let's call it ABCDEFG
2. Open your Gmail account for ABCDEFG, click on the upper right corner

3. Then click on PLAY GOOGLE DRIVE
4. You will be able to view all documents on the drive.

You can either save directly to your Google Drive or you can drag and drop documents.

This is perfect for people who travel or who like to work at home.

BACKUP — ONE OF YOUR # 1 PRIORITIES

In information technology, a backup, or the process of backing up, refers to the copying and archiving of computer data so it may be used to restore the original after a data loss event. We talked about backing up your phones but backing up your computer(s) is even more important because much of what you have on your computer is automatically shared with your phone.

I suggest that you have an IT person evaluate your computer system and make recommendations for what you need.

Most companies have an external backup system, such as an external hard drive. This is simply a box which is hooked up to your computer with a USB cord. Depending on what you purchase and how you set it up, it can backup daily, weekly or monthly. My IT person backs that up to a drive every few months.

We have a system called Carbonite (www.carbonite.com). Carbonite backs up as you are working. I love it because should anything happen, you can log in to Carbonite, view your files and restore them. It cannot get easier than that. Carbonite offers several packages; you can pick the one that is best for you.

Google Drive is also a cloud-storage backup. Here is a very interesting and informative article about using Google Drive as a backup. https://www.cloudwards.net/how-to-use-google-drive-to-backup-your-data/

Here's another useful article about backup from Blaze: https://www.backblaze.com/backup-your-computer.html

BACKUP IS YOUR #1 PRIORITY ...

ARE YOU PREPARED
FOR A MASSIVE AMOUNT
OF EMAIL AND TEXTING?

If you are not prepared for a whole lot of email and texting in your business, you better become prepared, because it is the way many people choose to do business.

If you are texting for business, you are not alone. In 2004, Americans sent 56 billion text messages according to Statista. By 2012, that figure was

2.109 billion. In fact, Americans send an average of 460 million mobile messages a month and not all of those are for personal communication. While roughly 269 billion emails were sent and received each day in 2017, the figure is expected to increase to almost 320 billion daily emails by 2021.

Not only your customers but also your vendors find it easier to send a quick email or text and they require a QUICK RESPONSE. For the most part it works, but sometimes people start emailing and texting and asking for quotes for numerous things, at which point I usually ask if it would be better to call them.

Below you will find guides to proper etiquette for texting and email. Avoid emojis, avoid cursing, avoid abbreviations, watch your tone—all pretty basic.

The most important thing I want to mention is - watch to whom you are sending a text. We are all in a hurry but this demands strict attention. Can you imagine anything worse than sending your friend an email about the horrible person you just did a job for but, by accident, that email or text goes to that horrible person you just did a job for? Names populate (automatically fill in) and it is an easy mistake to make, so my advice is to watch yourself, slow down a little, and be careful about the recipient to whom you are sending.

If you are employed by someone other than yourself, your employer has the right to read your email. Do not talk about work in a text or an email.

Many jobs have been lost when an employer sees that an employee is displeased with management or a co-worker or has done something wrong and covered it up. Your best choice is to keep text messages and emails brief and stick to general subjects, i.e., are you free for lunch next Tuesday or let's meet about our project tomorrow at 3.

The Ultimate Guide to Business Texting Etiquette:
https://www.textmagic.com/blog/ultimate-guide-to-business-texting- etiquette/

The Do's and Don'ts of Email Etiquette:
https://www.entrepreneur.com/article/272780

SOCIAL MEDIA

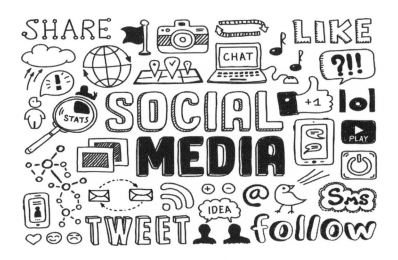

WARNING: SOCIAL MEDIA IS CRITICAL TO ANY BUSINESS, LARGE OR SMALL. WE WILL BE BRIEF ON THESE TOPICS BECAUSE THERE IS ENOUGH TO FILL A BOOK BY ITSELF. SO STAY TUNED FOR A FUTURE PUBLICATION FROM *MAKE YOUR BUSINESS OUR BUSINESS* **ON THIS RELEVANT TOPIC.**

It's 2018. You can spend lots of money for advertising, join several organizations, attend marketing events day and night, take people to lunch and even make speeches, but without a strong social media presence, you will get lost in the cracks.

Whether it's Facebook, LinkedIn, Twitter, Instagram, or Snapchat, people like to see the companies they are dealing with on these sites.

Some sites tend to be more personal, some more political, and some more professional. If it were not for LinkedIn, your co-authors would not have met and there would have been no opportunity for collaboration. Read a little about these sites. It may be time-consuming but if you are too busy working, you may neglect this very important ingredient in making your business successful.

FACEBOOK

Facebook is an online social networking website where people can create profiles, share information such as photos and quotes about themselves, and respond or link to the information posted by others.

Once you begin your notary business and you join Facebook, you will want to join several notary groups. You can connect with many people who will be happy to answer or discuss a question. You can also make your business a Facebook page where people can visit and see what you are doing. You can post articles and pictures. Be very careful about posting pictures of people without their consent. You might even have a consent form and have them sign off on it.

Since I do Apostilles in states throughout the country, if I need a notary in Illinois, it is an invaluable resource.

Below are some interesting facts: As of August, 2017:

- The total number of monthly active Facebook users was purported to be .01 billion;

- The total number of mobile monthly active Facebook users was purported to be 1.66 billion;

- The total number of desktop daily active Facebook users was purported to be 1.32 billion; and

- The total number of mobile daily active Facebook users was purported to be .57 billion.

LINKEDIN

By: Rose Carson/Shutterstock
www.linkedIn.com

LinkedIn is a social networking site designed specifically for the business community. The goal of the site is to allow registered members to establish networks with people they know and trust professionally. LinkedIn makes it easy to discover, connect and nurture relationships with people in the same business, search and apply for jobs, and get updates on topics and companies that make a difference to your business.

As of April 2017, LinkedIn had 500 million members in 200 countries, out of which more than 106 million members are active.

A basic membership in LinkedIn is free but there are some upgrades that charge a monthly fee. Network members are called "connections."

LinkedIn is where you want to post your resume, your accomplishments, and articles you think others might find relevant. For a notary, it is a site where you might seek out other notaries and do some cross-networking. As I mentioned before, LinkedIn is where your co-authors became connected and decided to collaborate on this book.

If you would like some additional coaching as to LinkedIn, email MakeYourBusinessOurBusiness and let's discuss.

TWITTER

By: Tanuha2001/Shutterstock
www.twitter.com

Twitter is a very popular social network and microblogging service that allows messages of only 280 characters or less. It's very simple to use as a broadcaster or a receiver. You can open a free account and select a Twitter name. Then you can send broadcasts as often as you like. You go to the 'What's Happening' box, type up to 280 characters, and click 'Tweet'. You might include some kind of media hyperlink, image, or video.

To receive Twitter feeds, you simply find someone interesting (celebrities included), and 'follow' them to subscribe to their tweets, or microblogs. If a person becomes uninteresting to you, you simply 'unfollow' them.

The message is probably called a "tweet" because it may remind you of the type of short and sweet chirp you might hear from a bird.

Here's a quick lesson on Twitter:
https://www.lifewire.com/what-exactly-is-twitter-2483331

INSTAGRAM

By: Estherpoon/Shutterstock
http://www.instagram.com/

Instagram is a social networking app made for sharing photos and videos from a smartphone. It›s known for its square image format and an assortment of interesting filters. Instagram uses a follower model just like Twitter. Similar to Facebook or Twitter, everyone who creates an *Instagram* account has a profile and a news feed. When you post a photo or video on *Instagram*, it will be displayed on your profile. The purpose of Instagram is to make connections with people who see the world in interesting ways. You can find and follow people based on images that inspire them, and if they like your photos, they'll follow you too.

Ten Instagram Tips for Beginners, from Lifewire:
https://www.lifewire.com/instagram-tips-for-beginners-3485872

BLOGGING

"Blog" is an abbreviated version of "weblog," a term used to describe websites that maintain an ongoing chronicle of information. A blog features diary-type commentary and links to articles on other websites, usually presented in reverse chronological order. Blogs range from the personal to the political, and can focus on one narrow subject or a whole range of subjects.

Many blogs focus on a particular topic but some are more eclectic, presenting links to all types of other sites. And others are more like personal journals, presenting the author's daily life and thoughts.

Generally speaking (although there are exceptions), blogs tend to have a few things in common:

- Amain content area with articles listed chronologically, newest on top
- An archive of older articles
- A way for people to leave comments about the articles
- A list of links to other related sites

A blog may sound much more complicated than it really is. A blog is just an idea – one which you want to share. Blogging was originally started so travelers could share their experiences but now it is largely so companies can share ideas with clients. Blogging is actually just posting material that will impress clients with your company's knowledge of different subjects. Blogging allows your clients to see that you are the "expert." If done correctly, it can build trust in you and your company.

The good news is that blogging is very easy to set up and somewhat affordable. There are free blog site options such as WordPress.com and Blogger, but to retain control and keep a professional image, we advise that you use your own domain name and host, and install WordPress or another content management system on your host. Most web hosts offer this option.

Search engine optimization rules the roost and is closely entwined with blogging. My blog is set so that if someone searches "Apostille" on the internet, my blog comes up as a result of that search.

One of the downsides of blogging is that it takes a lot of time and you have to keep up with it. Like Facebook and all social media, you don't want that search engine to tune into a blog that has not been updated in a year.

If you have no time to write an article, find an interesting relevant article and post it. Take some pictures or shoot a quick video ... anything to keep the momentum up.

CREATE A YOUTUBE CHANNEL

By: X9626/Shutterstock
www.youtube.com

With a Google Account, you can watch and like videos and subscribe to channels. However, without a YouTube channel, you have no public presence on YouTube. Even if you have a Google Account, you need to create a YouTube channel to upload videos, comment, or make playlists. You can use a computer or the YouTube mobile site to create a personal channel.

1. Sign in to YouTube on a computer or using the mobile site.

2. Then log in using the Google Account you'd like your channel to be associated with.

3. In the top right corner of the screen, click on your profile icon and then the 'Settings' cog icon.

4. Create a new channel by clicking Create a New Channel.

5. Next, you'll have the option to create a personal channel or a channel using a business or other name. Choose the business option.

6. Name your channel and select a category. The channel options available include:

   • Product or Brand

   • Company Institution or Organization

   • Arts, Entertainment or Sports

   • Other

7. Fill out the details to name your new channel and verify your account. Then, click Done. Congratulations! You've just created a new YouTube channel for your business.

SECTION III - TECHNOLOGY

Now that you have read this section, ask yourself the following questions. Daniel and Judith are available for questions and/or coaching at MakeYourBusinessOurBusiness@gmail.com.

1. Have you purchased the right equipment?
2. Have you made sure your printer is a dual-tray printer?
3. Have you studied the benefits of using Outlook?
4. Can you work from a remote location?
5. Have you studied using Google Drive?
6. Are you prepared with the proper backup?
7. Do you have someone who can assist you if your equipment goes south in the middle of a busy day?
8. Are you familiar with the many social media tools you can use?

DID YOU KNOW?

HERE ARE SOME PIECES OF INFORMATION THAT YOU WILL FIND USEFUL. THESE ARE SUBJECT TO CHANGE AND WE ENCOURAGE YOU TO CHECK WITH YOUR SPECIFIC STATE TO OBTAIN THEIR GUIDELINES...

WHICH STATES ARE AUTHORIZED TO CERTIFY COPIES OF DOCUMENTS?

Whether you are authorized to certify copies of documents depends on where you are commissioned. Most states permit it, but others states, including Alabama, Alaska, Illinois, Kentucky, Michigan, Mississippi, Nebraska, New Jersey, New York, North Carolina, Ohio, South Carolina, South Dakota and Tennessee, do not.

IN WHICH STATES CAN NOTARIES PERFORM MARRIAGES?

There are only three states that allow notaries to perform weddings. If you are a Florida, Maine, or South Carolina notary, you can solemnize a marriage or officiate at a wedding.

CAN YOU NOTARIZE DOCUMENTS IN A FOREIGN LANGUAGE?

Notaries are increasingly asked to notarize documents written in foreign languages they cannot read. Generally, state laws do not expressly prohibit the notary from notarizing a document that is not in the English language. However, depending on the circumstances, it may be inadvisable to notarize such foreign-language documents. The danger, of course, is that the document is being misrepresented to the notary.

For any non-English document, the best option is to refer the signer to a notary who reads and writes the language of the document. If that is not possible, the notary should only proceed if the notarial certificate itself is in English or other language the notary reads and writes. The letters and characters in the document's signature and in any ID document presented must also be understood by the notary.

It is important that the signer and the notary be able to communicate in the same language, without the reliance on a third party who, intentionally or unintentionally, may interpret the conversation or the document incorrectly.

CAN A NOTARY NOTARIZE FOR FAMILY MEMBERS?

A notary public who has a direct or indirect financial (or other beneficial) interest in a document may not notarize such a document. The better practice is not to notarize for a spouse or family member in order to preserve the integrity of the notarization and to prevent a challenge to the notarization.

WHICH STATES PERMIT REMOTE NOTARIZATION?

Some states such as Virginia, Ohio, and Montana will allow their commissioned notaries to remotely notarize documents from a web cam. In 2018, Texas and Nevada will also have remote notary laws that will go into effect.

HOW TO CHANGE YOUR NAME ON YOUR NOTARY COMMISSION

A notary public may change the name on his or her commission by sending the secretary of state a name change application (Form 2305), his or her

certificate of commission, a rider or endorsement from the insurance agency or surety showing the name change, and a $20 filing fee. This applies to all states.

HOW TO ORDER A NEW BIRTH CERTIFICATE / DEATH CERTIFICATE

If you have a request to order a new original Birth Certificate, the best way to do this online is www.vitalcheck.com. This is strictly a follow-the-prompts situation. A few tips:

Sometimes Vital Check will respond to your request and ask for additional pieces of information, perhaps a driver's license or affidavit of identity. Once they ask, that is the last time you will hear from them until the information is received. You must follow up yourself or it will be a month later and your client will not have his or her document(s).

Sometimes Vital Check has a backlog. Your request might be urgent in nature, someone needs to leave the country, or sometimes this is necessary for a cremation or burial. What you will need to do is get a signed, notarized statement of why this is urgent and fax it to them. Then you will have to call 24 hours later to make sure they received the fax.

Once you know they have the fax you will need to follow up every few hours until they have made a decision. Most of the time, if your document is specific and valid, they will approve your request and you will have the document in a couple of days.

You may also want to order the document through the Bureau of Vital Statistics or the Department of Health.

REQUESTING COPIES OF DEATH CERTIFICATES

State by State Death Certificate - https://www.everplans.com/articles/state-by-state-death-certificate-ordering-information

HOW TO CORRECT A BIRTH CERTIFICATE

You will need to check your local guidelines to do a correction on a birth certificate. Sometimes you need to contact the Department of Health, and sometimes it is called the Bureau of Vital Statistics.

HOW TO NOTARIZE IN A PRISON

A prison is not exactly the best place to visit, but sometimes notary services are requested.

One thing to remember: guests of the state typically have to surrender all of their normal forms of identification, such as driver's licenses, when they are incarcerated. This can be a problem if you show up for the notarization and the signer can't produce his or her identification. You need to know in advance if prison officials permit using the Credible Witness Rule.

A credible identifying witness is an individual who knows and can verify the identity of a signer. The witness appears at the time of the notarization and takes an oath or affirmation before the notary that the signer is who they claim to be, but lacks normal forms of ID.

Some states that require you to complete a journal entry, such as California, can make obtaining the inmate's signature or thumbprint more challenging. For example, you may have a sheet of Plexiglas or other barrier between you. You might not be allowed to hand a pen or journal to the signer directly, but may be required to give them to a guard who will hand them to the inmate. You will want to protect the privacy of unrelated journal entries when you hand off the journal to the inmate to sign, so be sure to attach a cover before handing the journal to the guard.

You should also know that your entire interaction with the inmate will be watched closely by one or more guards and your every word and move will be recorded on video.

HOW TO NOTARIZE FOR THE RICH AND FAMOUS

While it is fun to get a call from a baseball team or an actor or actress, remember that you have a responsibility to adhere to confidentiality. I have pictures of myself with some superstars but I have never pasted them on Facebook or Instagram, and when people see the pictures and ask about the details of the notary transaction, I do not answer the question.

WHY DO BANKS HIRE OUTSIDE NOTARIES?

Every so often a bank needs to examine safe deposit boxes that have not been looked at for a long period of time.

As a notary, you basically stand in the vault with a locksmith and a bank employee (usually a manager) while the locksmith opens the box. Sometimes the box is empty. If it is not empty, they will have to inventory the contents and pack them up to send to a central storage area and you will notarize the inventory sheet(s).

Because sometimes the boxes are empty, the assignment may be much shorter than originally planned. Make sure you arrange for what the fee will be fee in case you are there for one hour but they engaged you for the entire day.

WHAT IS A NOTARY AUTHENTICATION?

DO NOT CONFUSE THIS WITH A DOCUMENT AUTHENTICATION OR AN APOSTILLE. THIS IS A NOTARY AUTHENTICATION.

Every so often a client walks in with a document that is notarized and they have been told they have to get it notarized. What that means is they have to get the notary's signature authenticated.

Each state maintains a database of every commissioned notary. The client must take the document to the proper office. You will have to search for this information on your state's Secretary of State website. For a fee ($41.50 in PA) they will look up the notary and if the notary commission is authentic, they will stamp and seal the document accordingly.

WHAT STEPS MUST BE TAKEN WHEN A NOTARY DIES?

If your state doesn't provide rules for disposing of your notary seal and journal, you can follow <u>The Notary Public Code of Professional Responsibility</u>. It directs destroying or defacing the seal to ensure it cannot be misused. The *Code* directs keeping the journal in a secure place for at least 10 years from the date of the last entry, after which it can be destroyed.

It is not a pleasant thought, but you should arrange for the commissioning official in your state to be notified of your death. California, Mississippi and New Mexico are among the states that require the Secretary of State to be notified. Mississippi has a specific form that must be completed for this purpose. You could place a blank form in a file or provide instructions for where to download the form.

Here are some examples:

Arizona requires a notary seal and journals that contain only public records to be delivered by certified mail to the Secretary of State's office within three months of a notary's death. Arizona has different rules for journals that include public and non-public records. A notary's journal that includes records that violate the attorney-client privilege or that are confidential under federal or Arizona law (such as records related to an abortion) becomes the property of the notary's employer and must be retained by the employer until five years after the date of the last record in the journal, after which the journal may be destroyed. Failure of a personal representative to properly dispose of the seal and journal is punishable by a $50-$500 fine.

California requires the personal representative of the notary to promptly deliver all notarial records to the office of the county clerk in which the notary's oath of office is filed. The representative must destroy or deface the deceased notary's seal so that it cannot be taken and used by another person.

Florida only requires a notary to have a seal, but not a journal. Its law therefore only addresses the seal, which must be destroyed when a notary's commission permanently ends, unless the Governor specifically requests the seal be turned in.

Hawaii requires a deceased notary's representative to deliver the notary's seal and journal to the state attorney general's office within 90 days of the notary's death.

Texas requires a deceased notary's record books and public papers to be turned in to the county clerk's office of the county where the notary resided. The notary's seal should be destroyed to prevent misuse by another individual.

In the wrong hands, a notary's seal can be used by criminals to forge a phony notarization on important documents, and a journal of notarial acts may contain personal information about signers that can be used to commit identity theft. That's why you should leave instructions to ensure that your tools are not carelessly thrown away or left where someone might take them. Many states have provisions regarding this situation.

SECTION IV – DID YOU KNOW

Now that you have read this section, ask yourself the following questions. Daniel and Judith are available for questions and/or coaching at MakeYourBusinessOurBusiness@gmail.com.

1. Did you know which states are authorized to certify copies of documents?
2. Did you know in which states can notaries perform marriages?
3. Did you know if you can notarize documents in a foreign language?
4. Did you know if a notary can notarize for family members?
5. Did you know which states permit remote notarization?
6. Did you know how to change your name on your notary commission?
7. Did you know how to order a new Birth Certificate / Death Certificate?
8. Did you know how to correct a Birth Certificate?
9. Did you know how to notarize in a prison?
10. Did you know how to notarize for the rich and famous?
11. Did you know why Banks hire outside notaries?
12. Did you know what a Notary Authentication is?
13. Did you know what steps must be taken when a notary dies?

ESTATE PLANNING DOCUMENTS

SOME TIPS ON SIGNING ESTATE DOCUMENTS

ALWAYS SUGGEST THAT THESE DOCUMENTS BE REVIEWED BY AN ATTORNEY. NEVER VOLUNTEER WHAT YOU MIGHT THINK IS RIGHT OR WRONG. THESE DOCUMENTS WILL AFFECT PEOPLE FOR YEARS TO COME.

NOTARIZING LAST WILLS
AND TESTAMENTS

by American Association of Notaries

Use this information as your guidelines if you wish to accept these types of assignments. This is state-specific so be sure to research your own state's rules and regulations.

Wills are highly sensitive probate documents that determine how a person's assets will be distributed after his or her death. The person making the will is called a "testator" if male and a "testatrix" if female.

Some states advise novice notaries against notarizing wills unless those notaries are knowledgeable about the practice. Many notaries who encounter wills, do so within the capacity of their occupation, for instance as a legal assistant or an employee of a law firm that handles wills and other estate-planning documents. Such wills are drafted by attorneys with specific instructions and pre-printed notarial certificates for the notary to complete.

Problems can arise when a client presents a notary with a self-prepared will and the client depends on the notary to determine the appropriate notarial certificate. In such cases, a savvy notary should decline to perform the notarial act and advise the person to contact an attorney for advice. You might also suggest that investing in a good attorney will prevent problems down the road with contested wills or wills thrown out in probate court due to sloppy execution procedures.

Laws regarding the proper execution of wills vary greatly from state to state. In states such as New York and North Carolina, a will does not have to be notarized to be accepted for probate in the courts. However, attorneys in those states recommend drafting "self-proving wills" to speed up the probate. A "self-proving will" is one in which the testator and the disinterested witnesses swear, in an affidavit in front of a notary, that the testator is fully aware of what is being signed and that the disinterested witnesses witnessed the testator sign the will. In these states, the court will accept "self-proving wills" without contacting the witnesses who witnessed the testator sign the will. In the absence of a self-proving will, it will be necessary to track down the original witnesses to "prove" he or she witnessed the signing of the will, which can be difficult and time-consuming for the heirs.

In California, a will only needs the signatures of two disinterested witnesses who witness the testator sign the will and does not need to be notarized in order to be valid. In some states, such as Texas, a holographic will (written entirely in the testator's own handwriting) is considered valid. It would be prudent, therefore, for the notary in those states to make it a practice to refuse to notarize hand-written wills and to refer clients with those requests to an attorney.

In conclusion, notaries should exercise caution when notarizing wills. Because of a lack of understanding and diligence, an improperly drafted will that is notarized can be declared null. If you are not comfortable with notarizing a will, you should not proceed. If you have questions, politely ask the client to contact his or her lawyer who drafted the will.

One last note: always follow the steps for proper notarization when performing notarial acts by requesting the physical presence of the signer, properly identifying the signer and ensuring that the signer is competent and fully understands what is being signed.

I NEED A WITNESS

Witnesses are neutral third parties whose job is to ensure that the document was signed by both parties and no forgery took place. Having someone there to attest to this can be valuable if there is ever a dispute regarding the parties or the contract. Witnesses may also confirm the identity of both parties. They then sign the document as a witness to prove they saw each party sign.

It is important to note that witnesses cannot benefit from the contract in any way or be related to one of the parties. For instance, a beneficiary cannot witness a will where they will be inheriting assets.

In addition, witnesses must be 18 years old and of sound mind when witnessing a document's execution.

I am frequently asked whether a notary can serve as a witness. Most jurisdictions allow a notary to serve as a witness. But if they are witnessing a document, they cannot verify their own signature as a notary because it would be a conflict of interest.

As a notary, whenever you are executing a document, you need to make sure you are signing the document in accordance with your state law's requirements and those of your document. You must also be certain to get proper identification from the witness(es) and keep a record of it in your journal.

WHAT IS A POWER OF ATTORNEY?

Powers of Attorney are critical documents and I encourage clients to have these documents drafted by an attorney. I carefully explain to them that I would not be able to give them legal advice.

Briefly, a Power of attorney ("POA") is a written authorization to represent or act on another's behalf in private affairs, business, or some other legal matter. The person authorizing the other to act is the principal, grantor, or donor (of the "power"). The person who will carry out the duties authorized in the POA is known as the "agent." The agent must sign the Power of Attorney authorizing his or her acceptance of the duties outlined in the document.

An ordinary power of attorney is effective only when the principal has the legal capacity to act. When the principal becomes unable to communicate, an ordinary power of attorney is no longer legally effective.

The Durable Power of Attorney is much more encompassing. It does not have a set time period and it becomes effective immediately after the incapacitation of the principal. It does expire upon the principal's death except for acts of funeral arrangements or the donation of organs.

WHAT IS A CREDIBLE WITNESS?

A credible identifying witness is an individual who knows and can verify the identity of a signer. The witness appears at the time of the notarization and takes an oath or affirmation before the notary that the signer is who they claim to be but lacks other forms of ID. Essentially, a credible identifying witness serves as a human ID card for the signer.

This is something that you need to check with your local state guidelines. For example, Virginia does not allow the use of credible witnesses.

If this is a jail signing, inmates never have an acceptable ID unless it is handed to them by a visitor. When doing a jail signing, an attorney or a family member will normally meet the notary. You must make sure that the ID is current and state-issued.

There is no such thing as a credible witness notary, but you can be a notary who uses a credible witness. Just make sure you know the number of witnesses that a particular state allows.

This is not a black and white issue and as a notary you may need to seek out assistance on a case-by-case basis.

VI. EMPLOYMENT DOCUMENTS

I-9 VERIFICATION

The 1-9 Verification Form, issued by the U.S. Citizenship and Immigration Services (USCIS) verifies the identity and employment eligibility for employees hired in the United States. The form must be completed by both the employee and the employer (or authorized representative). As part of the process, the employee must submit documents evidencing his or her identity and/or eligibility to work in the United States, and the employer (or authorized representative) must physically examine said documents. According to the USCIS Handbook for Employers, employers may designate someone to fill out Forms 1-9 for you, such as a notary public.

No seal or stamp may be used to authenticate these documents. While this is not a notarial act, the Notary should record the transaction including the name of the employee, the name of the company requesting the authentication or completion of Section 2, and the date he or she completed the transaction.

You should check your state guidelines as certain states have certain restrictions for performing I-9 Verifications.

Please note:

".... It should be clear that while a notary may sign on behalf of an employer, the notary does not do so in the capacity of a notary public under the Notary Public Law but rather as an agent of the employer. Thus, the notary may convey that he or she is an agent for the employer in the 'Title of Employer or Authorized Representative box in Section 2 of the I-9. However, no notary title or seal should be used to complete the I-9 as an authorized representative of the employer. "Pennsylvania Notaries and Completion of I-9 Forms"; revised March 2013). (National Notary Association Website)

VII. INSURANCE

PROTECTING YOUR NOTARY BUSINESS

Having the proper protection for your notary business is critical for the basic operation of your business. Each state has certain requirements. In Indiana, for example, notaries are required to have, as of this writing, a $5,000 bond. On July 1, 2018, the bond requirement will be

$25,000 for an eight-year term. In Pennsylvania, the bond requirement is $10,000. This is why you should check the reference websites in the back of this book for your specific state to ensure you understand how much of a bond your state requires for you as a notary public.

Please keep in mind bonds actually protect the public and not the notary. That means if there is ever an issue and your bond is called in to pay damages, the notary would need to repay the bond back to the bonding company. The bond is required in most jurisdictions for this reason—to make sure consumers in that jurisdiction have a way of collecting any damages through a notarial transaction.

Ok, I now have a notary bond. Can I go out and start taking assignments and conduct transactions? Do I have everything I need to be properly insured?

The answer is NO. To properly ensure that your notary business is protected from loss, the notary entrepreneur needs a few more items of insurance. Please keep in mind that when you conduct daily transactions, by the end of most weeks you will have facilitated transactions on millions of dollars of assets. In most cases the notary will be meeting each participant in the transaction for the first time at the transaction. To properly cover your business, we recommend additional insurance coverage.

WARNING: SAFETY IS VERY IMPORTANT. If you feel in any way that you are walking into a dangerous situation, do not do it!

ERRORS AND OMISSIONS
INSURANCE (E&O)

As a notary entrepreneur, you want to protect yourself from the unexpected. Notary E&O Insurance is designed to protect you, the notary entrepreneur. Unintentional mistakes or a false claim against you could cost you thousands of dollars to defend yourself in a lawsuit. Even if you were employed by and acting as a notary public for that employer, you shouldn't assume that your employer has proper E&O Insurance coverage for you. The general public can come after you individually as a notary as well as your employer for unintended mistakes.

Why do I need this extra E&O Insurance when I have a notary bond?

If a claim is made against your bond, you are required by law to pay it back.

Keep in mind your notary bond is not your insurance protection. The notary bond is designed to protect the general public and not you, the notary entrepreneur. According to the National Notary Association, "Your bond protects the public from financial harm that results from any negligent mistake or intentional misconduct you commit while performing a notarization."

You could also be held personally responsible for any additional cost above the amount of your bond which might include court costs, legal fees, and other expenses. This is why having notary errors and omission insurance is designed to protect you.

Your E&O Insurance will pay your legal defense by an attorney and your legal fees and court costs with no deductible and no replacement of losses.

Consider these actual cases cited by the National Notary Association:

A property owner and a bank filed a lawsuit against a notary alleging negligence in the notarization process that cost them substantial sums of money. Although the notary had done nothing wrong in the transaction, unbeknownst to her, she had been deceived by identity thieves. The notary ultimately chose to pay money to settle both lawsuits rather than endure the unpleasantness and added financial burden of prolonged litigation. E & O Insurance would have protected her.

Several lawsuits were filed against a notary alleging that some of the signatures she had notarized were forgeries, even though she was assured by her boss that they were okay. Without E&O Insurance, and unprotected by her company's policy, the notary was forced to file personal bankruptcy rather than try to defend the lawsuits.

A bank filed a lawsuit against a notary claiming that an unpaid, uncollectible loan was due to the negligence of the notary for the apparent notarization of a forged signature. The notary immediately contacted his Errors & Omissions Insurance carrier, cooperated with the carrier's defense of the lawsuit and it was ultimately settled by the carrier within the limit of the policy. The notary was not held liable for any out-of-pocket costs associated with the matter, nor was he inconvenienced with added work, the E&O Insurance carrier handled the matter for him.

VII. HOW TO BECOME
A CERTIFIED SIGNING AGENT

To become a Certified Notary Signing Agent, you must be a commissioned notary public and pass a Notary Signing Agent background screening and certification exam. The certification is required by most lenders, signing services and title companies, before they will assign a notary any work. This procedure is state specific so be sure you choose the state of your commission before you begin this process. In the next chapter, *"Professional Notary Signing Companies"* deals with contacting these companies to obtain work.

Once you sign up and select a package, the company you choose will immediately process your background screening. That takes a few days and once completed, you will receive an email notifying you about the examination.

You should DEFINITELY complete the online training before you begin the testing. And don't be afraid of the examination because you can take it more than once until you pass.

You will need to take this test every year to maintain your certification. In the interim, you can also learn a lot about this through 123 Notary. (http://www.123notary.com/certified-signing-agent.asp)

Happy Testing!!!

PROFESSIONAL SIGNING COMPANIES

Why does a title company use a professional signing company rather than call a notary for a closing?

A professional signing company takes the heat. They take the responsibility of screening the notary for credentials; they do the scheduling; they handle getting the documents to the notary; if a notary cancels at the last minute, it is up to them to find a replacement; and they handle the invoicing. It is a domino effect; the lender hires the professional signing company, the professional signing company hires the notary. That is why you will sometimes see a fee on the closing disclosure for $225, but the notary only gets $100; there is a fee for the professional signing company and a fee for the lender.

Once you make a connection, if you follow the instructions below, you will have yourself a new client.

HOW YOU GET ASSIGNMENTS

The signing company calls or emails you to ascertain your availability for a specific appointment. Especially in the beginning, you will need to respond almost immediately. Once they get to know you and like your work, they will wait a few minutes but keep in mind a busy scheduler wants to get your appointment set up and move to the next one.

At that time, they will give you information on the type of signing, the location, and the fee they agree to pay you. Here I offer a word of caution: think for a moment before you say yes. Is the location somewhere accessible to me? If I have any doubt, I use the zip code calculator on my phone and see how long the trip will take me. I also consider the time of day; will I be on the expressway right in the middle of rush-hour traffic? Is the fee enough to compensate me for the time? And if I already have a closing scheduled, do I have enough time to get from one place to another and be on time for both appointments? Being on time is important; if you want this signing company to continue to give you work, you <u>must</u> make sure they have no complaints about you.

YOU ACCEPT THE ASSIGNMENT

Once you accept the assignment, you in most instances will receive a signing confirmation which contains the logistics of the closing and the name, address, and telephone number of the signer(s). You will need to confirm the appointment.

CONFIRMING THE APPOINTMENT.

I make it a practice to do this as soon as I receive the confirmation. It takes less than two minutes:

1. Introduce yourself. "My name is Judith and I am going to be your notary on Tuesday for your refinance. I just wanted to confirm the logistics with you; I am coming to 123 Main Street at 6:30 PM."

2. Once the person says that the logistics are correct, you say," Please make sure you and your spouse have a valid photo ID. I will need to take a copy of it."

3. If the person says, "I am going to be at my brother's; could you come there instead" you must let the signing company know of the change of address.

Then go back to the email and reply APPOINTMENT CONFIRMED.

RECEIVING DOCUMENTS AND DIRECTIONS

When you receive the confirmation or the documents, you will receive instructions. This is a challenge because all of them are different and all of them are formatted differently. If you want to get financially compensated for the job, you are required to follow the directions. Keep a copy with the documents. I use a yellow highlighter for the things I want to make sure not to forget. The instructions might tell you:

- the documents must be signed in blue or black ink
- they need two copies of the closing disclosure
- they sometimes need two copies of ID rather than just one
- especially if you are signing at night, you will have a number to call in case the signer has a problem
- look for time deadlines – often they want documents within 24 hours

They will give you instructions as to the documents – you might have to scan certain documents before you send the package back. In certain instances, you might have to scan the package and wait for funding approval before anyone leaves the closing.

Finally, they will give you someone to call, text or email when the closing is completed. This is a critical instruction because you are letting them know their client's job has been completed.

REMEMBER, the devil is in the details, and if you follow the instructions and take care of the details, the signing company will remember, and they will call you again.

WHAT CREDENTIALS YOU WILL NEED

In almost all instances now you will be signing up to work for these professional signing companies online. You will follow the prompts. You should have the following documents saved on your desktop for uploading:

- Notary Commission
- Background Screening
- Bond (if applicable)
- Insurance
- Signing Agent Certification
- W-9

WHAT ARE THE PITFALLS?

To me, the only pitfall of doing this kind of work is that if you do not follow the specific instructions, you will not be called back. Understand that the professional signing company is working for their client and wants to make sure their client is pleased and if they can count on you for that, your phone will ring the next time they have work in your area.

DEEDS

Deeds must be executed carefully as they are "recordable documents" which means that they will need to be filed with the Recorder of Deeds.

As a notary, you are concerned with authenticating the signer of the deed. Here is where it can get tricky. If below or above the signature line there is additional verbiage, the deed will have to be signed that way. Here is an example:

Mary Jones, Administratrix of the Estate of
Edward J. Jones, Jr.

_____

This deed will need to be signed by Mary Jones, Administratrix of the Estate of Edward J. Jones, Jr.

A notary should always ask the person signing the deed to date the deed in his or her own handwriting. A deed is a recordable document and if the date shown is not today's date, the notary cannot notarize it. The Recorder of Deeds won't accept it.

DEED PACKAGES

It's a trend. Just imagine your grandparents not attending their real estate closing. Times have changed. Now we have people who are traveling through Philadelphia (my city) for business or pleasure and have a mortgage closing back home in Louisiana, which needs to be signed within a specific period of time to keep the transaction rate locked in.

Sometimes they only need to sign a Power of Attorney allowing their designated representative to handle the closing on their behalf. Sometimes they need to sign all of the closing documents and have them sent back by overnight mail. This scenario happens to the general population, attorneys, athletes, actors and actresses, and many more. Such assignments are almost always at the last minute. Just recently I signed a Power of Attorney for a famous athlete at a popular Italian restaurant on a Friday night at 8:00 P.M. so that it could be scanned for a Saturday afternoon closing.

A good signer will go through the documents and show the clients where ALL the documents need to be signed, not just the ones that need to be notarized. It is important that these documents are signed and notarized correctly because failure to do that could hold up the closing.

NOTE: If a client brings this package to you and allows you to look only at what he or she thinks needs notarization, I suggest you put that information in your journal notes, because if there were other documents that needed attention and the closing does not happen, it will be your fault that the package was signed incorrectly.

SECTION VII - HOW TO BECOME A CERTIFIED NOTARY SIGNING AGENT

Now that you have read this section, ask yourself the following questions. Daniel and Judith are available for questions and/or coaching at MakeYourBusinessOurBusiness@gmail.com.

1. Have you taken the necessary steps in your specific state to become a Certified Notary Signing Agent ("CNSA")?

2. Have you completed your testing?

3. Have you downloaded your CNSA Certification?

4. Have you researched professional signing companies in your state who use CNSAs?

5. Have you made sure you have all the necessary credentials?

6. Have you practiced a few times or shadowed a more experienced signer?

IX. HOW TO BECOME A MOBILE SIGNING AGENT

Offering mobile notary service is an excellent way to generate revenue for your company. You will receive calls from attorneys, physicians, hospitals and nursing homes, prisons, and the general population.

Years ago we would have suggested that you write letters to hospitals and nursing homes, introducing yourself and enclosing a business card. Today it is all about the internet. If you have a good presence on the internet and you have joined some websites, your phone will ring.

It is very important that you are familiar with the rules regarding signings before you begin to take on this kind of work. You need to familiarize yourself with witnessing, and in particular, the credible witness rules. Think about a beautician who gets a job in a high-priced salon but he or she has not really practiced doing hair. The first few people he or she served were notterribly happy and in fact, made some comments to the manager. So the beautician never really had a chance. The opposite might have been true if he or she had spent some time and practiced before jumping in.

I do a lot of mobile work and a high percentage of it is repeat business. Here are some tips for a mobile notary signer:

1. Make sure you confirm the appointment.
2. Anyone who is signing a document will need to present a valid item of photo ID. That includes witnesses. Sometimes signing companies require two forms of Identification and it is important that the client be prepared. Passports are acceptable identification (except if this is a PennDOT (Pennsylvania) transaction, as they do not accept passports as identification).
3. It is recommended that notaries obtain an identification card stating that they are a commissioned notary with a photo ID. That is a layer of protection for the notary, so you are not giving out personal information.
4. Make sure you bring pens with you, both blue and black.

5. If the client has documents, make sure they know that they should <u>not</u> sign the document(s) until you are there.

6. Make sure you have good directions and alternate routes to get to your destination in case you encounter traffic problems.

7. Dress professionally. No jeans, no sneakers.

8. If this signing is for someone who is undergoing treatment at a hospital, nursing home, hospice, rehabilitation, etc., please make sure someone has that person's identification available at the time of the signing. In addition, make sure that witnesses are available if they are going to be required.

WARNING: SAFETY IS VERY IMPORTANT. If you feel in any way that you are walking into a dangerous situation, do not do it!

I recently received a call on a Sunday afternoon. The man said he was desperate and offered me a great deal of money to come and notarize a separation agreement. When I arrived, he and his wife were yelling at each other. In a polite way, I said that if they were going to be fighting I was going to be leaving, and she said, "That's a good idea." I walked out the door and never looked back because the atmosphere in that house was frightening and I did not want to be in the middle of a physical marital dispute.

Here are a few tips for a situation such as this: In a separation and/or divorce request for signing, first, if you have an office, have them come to your office. If you do not have an office, it is probably a better idea to meet in a public place. The posture will be different and the signing is more likely to occur.

In a situation like this, accept payment for the time it took you to travel to the signing.

If you have any doubt as to the particular neighborhood or house, find a Starbucks or a Dunkin' Donuts and meet your client there.

Be aware of ANIMALS. I am not comfortable around very large dogs. Daniel once went into a home with over 30 birds in a small space. Daniel needed medical treatment and had temporary asthma as a result of this situation and needed almost two weeks to recuperate from the experience.

Always be friendly but don't be afraid to protect yourself at all costs.

Especially when I was starting my business, I would tell someone where I was heading and approximately when I would be returning. It's always a good idea for someone to know where you are.

YOUR NOTARY TOOLBOX

To be a successful mobile notary signer, you must be armed with a toolbox so that whatever you need, you have. Different notaries do it differently but there are just certain tools that are mandatory to carry with you.

I probably do not have to say this but you will need your smartphone. It is important that you be able to get directions including an alternate route in case you run into a detour. Some notaries carry an alternate phone "just in case."

Next would be the instructions. Whether you have received instructions from a title company or you have instructions from the person whom you are visiting, you should print out your instructions including the telephone number where you are expected to be. If this is a title company or a lender, and particularly if the signing takes place in the evening, many times these instructions include a telephone number of someone to call if there is a problem at the table.

I make it a practice to call even if I am going to be 5 minutes late. Sometimes people say "no worries, I'm not going anywhere so take your time." Other times this appointment has been carefully scheduled around work, childcare, and/or another appointment and letting them know that you are almost there makes them feel better and they are not annoyed before you even get started.

It goes without saying that you must have your **seal** and stamp.

Believe it or not, another primary suggestion is to have several pens. Nothing like being seated at the head of the table and then having to search for pens. Some signings require you to only use blue ink and some ask for black so it is my suggestion that you carry both.

It is always a good idea to have an acknowledgment and a jurat in your bag should you need one.

Although this is off the subject … the instructions almost always give you a number to call when the signing has been completed. Usually, someone is checking to make sure the signings have been done and if they don't hear from you, they have to call you. The next time they are assigning work they will remember the notary who has followed instructions.

SECTION VIII - HOW TO BECOME A MOBILE SIGNING AGENT

Now that you have read this section, ask yourself the following questions. Daniel and Judith are available for questions and/or coaching at MakeYourBusinessOurBusiness@gmail.com.

1. Have you made sure you have reliable transportation?

2. Have you made sure you have a reliable GPS and Map system?

3. Have you made sure you have appropriate notary credentials?

4. Is your Notary Toolbox in order?

ABOUT THE AUTHOR –
DANIEL C. LEWIS

Daniel C. Lewis is an entrepreneur, writer, video editor, and Managing Partner of Lewis Notary Services Inc. He was named the 2010 Notary of the Year by the National Notary Association. He is also the founder of Lewis Training Service. Daniel has a legal background working as a paralegal for local attorneys. He has extensive experience as a Senior Loan Officer and as a Senior Mortgage Broker. Daniel has presented workshops all over the country on effective and efficient business practices.

Daniel is an Approved Instructor for the Indiana Department of Insurance on continuing education courses for notaries and also the current President of the Indiana Notary Association. As President of the Indiana Notary Association, Daniel has successfully lobbied to improve the office of the notary public by testifying during Senate and General Assembly hearings, resulting in raising the standards for notaries throughout Indiana.

ABOUT THE AUTHOR – JUDITH LAWRENCE

Judith Lawrence is the owner and operator of Notary Service 100, LLC, and Center City Notary, LLC. She is a Certified Notary Signing Agent, a Certified Apostille Agent, and a Full Auto Tags Agent for the state of Pennsylvania.

Judith worked as a legal secretary for several years in the real estate, mortgage, and tax departments. She credits this experience for the successful notary and signing company she has built. Judith worked for such prestigious firms as Fellheimer & Eichen, Ballard Spahr, and Montgomery McCracken.

She brings a great deal of longevity, as well as experience, to this business.

Judith is a member of the National Notary Association, the American Association of Notaries, and the Pennsylvania Association of Notaries. She is also active in the Philadelphia Area Concierge Association. She is on the Board of Elections for the State of Pennsylvania. She has served on several diversity committees and is active in a number of community organizations.

Judith enjoys public speaking and is focusing on coaching others as to how to reinvent a career.

CERTIFIED NOTARY
SIGNING AGENT

Once you have established yourself as a notary public, you will probably want to take the next step and become a Certified Notary Signing Agent. This will certify you to conduct mortgage closings on behalf of lenders and title companies. We have briefly touched on this, but our next book will give you much more detailed information on how to do this.

APOSTILLES

Apostille is a French word meaning "certification." An Apostille is a certification provided under The Hague Convention of 1961 for authenticating documents for use in foreign countries. It is issued by the

U.S. Secretary of State. The sole function is to verify the authenticity of the signature of the document. An Apostille is simply a certificate that is attached to another document so that it will be accepted when used overseas. If the country of destination of the Apostille does not participate in The Hague Convention, documents being sent to that country can be "authenticated" or "certified". In the United States, all 50 states and the Federal Government (U.S. Department of State – Office of Authentication) can issue an Apostille.

The Apostille Convention requires that all Apostilles be numbered consecutively, with individual numbers applied to each Apostille issued. The recognized standard Apostille contains a seal and 10 mandatory references: name of the country from which the document emanates, name of the person signing the document, the capacity in which the person signing the document has acted, in the case of unsigned documents, the name of the authority that has affixed the seal or stamp, place of certification date of certification, the authority issuing the certificate, number of certificates, seal or stamp of authority issuing certificate and signature of authority issuing certificate.

A Certified Apostille Agent is a notary trained and certified to correctly and promptly obtain the required government authentications from the proper county, state, federal, and embassy government authorities in the correct order for documents to be presented in foreign countries. The agent is trained in what is required, where to go, what to do and how to correctly expedite the process as promptly as possible. The physical application of the required apostille/certification seal is placed by a U.S. Designated Competent Authority. The Certified Apostille Agent serves as a professional fee-paid agent for individuals, schools, corporations, etc. needing authentications for these documents to be presented in foreign counties.

This is a complicated but very interesting business because you will have clients who need certifications throughout the United States and all over the world. Many times you will need to research to find out the requirements of different states and various countries. For example, in Pennsylvania the documents come back with a yellow seal; some state seals are red, and some states have no seal.

For more information including upcoming webinars, check out Centercitynotary.com.

AUTO TAGS

I am a full agent with PennDOT, the Pennsylvania Department of Transportation.

There are many things to consider before you start an agency; there is an investment of time to learn the business, plus you will need licensing fees, a bond and supplies. This work is state specific. You will need to take an on-line basic agent service training course which has been approved by your state's department of transportation. You will need to do your research and see what the requirements are for your state. In my case, the excellent support desk at the Pennsylvania Association of Notaries was invaluable in my learning process. I couldn't have come this far without them.

This business is very intense. It takes some serious learning of not only the mechanics of being an agent but the forms and the rules that go along with it. I highly recommend doing it. I also recommend doing it with someone else so two people can learn together and back each other up on evenings and weekends.

FINANCIAL PLANNING

Did you ever ask yourself these questions? How much income do I need to make t be respected as a business owner? How can I earn additional income and manage my expenses effectively? How do I consolidate debt and strive to eliminate it, all at the same time? How much is enough income to properly prepare for unexpected expenses? How do I build up enough wealth to outpace inflation and to legally, morally, and ethically reduce taxation? How do I properly build and preserve my family legacy?

To get these questions answered and more, look for our next book, MakeYourBusinessOurBusiness – Financial Planning.

REFERENCES

WHAT LAW GOVERNS NOTARIZATION THROUGHOUT THE UNITED STATES

Throughout this book, in many instances we tell you that you must check with your specific state to validate how certain things need to be done and that certain forms that might be different from state to state. However, below is the governing law allowing you to act as a notary public throughout the USA.

- **10 U.S. Code § 1044a - Authority to act as notary**

US Code	Notes
(a)	The persons named in subsection (b) have the general powers of a notary public and of a consul of the United States in the performance of all notarial acts to be executed by any of the following:
(1)	Members of any of the armed forces.
(2)	Other persons eligible for legal assistance under the provisions of section 1044 of this title or regulations of the Department of Defense.
(3)	Persons serving with, employed by, or accompanying the armed forces outside the United States and outside the Commonwealth of Puerto Rico, Guam, and the Virgin Islands.
(4)	Other persons subject to the Uniform Code of Military Justice (chapter 47 of this title) outside the United States. (b)Persons with the powers described in subsection (a) are the following:
(1)	All judge advocates, including reserve judge advocates when not in a duty status.
(2)	All civilian attorneys serving as legal assistance attorneys.

(3)	All adjutants, assistant adjutants, and personnel adjutants, including reserve members when not in a duty status.
(4)	All other members of the armed forces, including reserve members when not in a duty status, who are designated by regulations of the armed forces or by statute to have those powers.
(5)	For the performance of notarial acts at locations outside the United States, all employees of a military department or the Coast Guard who are designated by regulations of the Secretary concerned or by statute to have those powers for exercise outside the United States.
(6)	All civilian paralegals serving at military legal assistance offices, supervised by a military legal assistance counsel (as defined in section 1044d(g) of this title).
(c)	No fee may be paid to or received by any person for the performance of a notarial act authorized in this section.
(d)	The signature of any such person acting as notary, together with the title of that person's offices, is prima facie evidence that the signature is genuine, that the person holds the designated title, and that the person is authorized to perform a notarial act.

(Added Pub. L. 101–510, div. A, title V, § 551(a)(1), Nov. 5, 1990, 104 Stat. 1566; amended Pub. L. 104–201, div. A, title V, § 573, Sept. 23, 1996, 110 Stat. 2534; Pub. L. 107–107, div. A, title XI, § 1103, Dec. 28, 2001, 115 Stat. 1236; Pub. L. 114–328, div. A, title V, § 523(b), Dec. 23, 2016, 130 Stat. 2116.)

SPECIFIC STATE INFORMATION
FOR NOTARIES

CALIFORNIA

The California Secretary of State, Notary Public & Special Filings Section, is responsible for appointing and commissioning qualified persons as notaries public for four-year terms.

Prior to sitting for the notary exam, one must complete a mandatory six-hour course of study. This required course of study is conducted either in an online, home study, or in-person format via an approved notary education vendor. Both prospective notaries as well as current notaries seeking reappointment must undergo an "expanded" FBI and California Department of Justice background check.

Various statutes, rules, and regulations govern notaries public. California law sets maximum, but not minimum, fees for services related to notarial acts (e.g., per signature: acknowledgment $15, jurat $15, certified power of attorney $15, et cetera). A fingerprint (typically the right thumb) may be required in the notary journal based on the transaction in question (e.g., deed, quitclaim deed, deed of trust affecting real property, power of attorney document, et cetera). Documents with blank spaces cannot be notarized (a further anti-fraud measure). California explicitly prohibits notaries public from using literal foreign language translation of their title. The use of a notary seal is required.

COLORADO

Notarial acts performed in Colorado are governed under the Notaries Public Act, 12-55-101, et seq. Pursuant to the Act, notaries are appointed by the Secretary of State for a term not to exceed four years. Notaries may apply for appointment or reappointment online at the Secretary of State's website. A notary may apply for reappointment to the notary office 90 days before her commission expires. Beginning in early 2010, all new notaries will be required to take a training course and pass an examination to ensure minimal competence of the Notaries Public Act. A course of instruction approved by the Secretary of State may be administered by approved vendors and shall bear an emblem with a certification number assigned by the Secretary of State's office. An approved course of instruction covers relevant provisions of the Colorado Notaries Public Act, the Model Notary Act, and widely accepted best practices. In addition to courses offered by approved vendors, the Secretary of State offers free certification courses at the Secretary of State's office. To sign up for a free course, visit the notary public training page at the following link. A third party seeking to verify the status of a Colorado notary may do so by visiting the Secretary of State's website at the following link. Constituents seeking an apostille or certificate of magistracy are requested to complete the form found on the following page before sending in their documents or presenting at the Secretary of State's office.

FLORIDA

Florida notaries public are appointed by the Governor to serve a four-year term. New applicants and commissioned notary public must be bona fide residents of the State of Florida and first-time applicants must complete a mandatory three-hour education course administered by an approved educator. Florida state law also requires that a notary public post bond in the amount of $7,500.00. A bond is required to compensate an individual harmed because of a breach of duty by the notary. Applications are submitted and processed through an authorized bonding agency. Florida is one of three states (Maine and South Carolina are the others) where a notary public can solemnize the rites of matrimony (perform a marriage ceremony).

The Department of State appoints civil law notaries, also called "Florida International Notaries", who must be Florida attorneys who have practiced law for five or more years. Applicants must attend a seminar and pass an exam administered by the Department of State or any private vendor approved by the department. Such civil law notaries are appointed for life and may perform all the acts of a notary public in addition to preparing authentic acts.

ILLINOIS

Notaries public in Illinois are appointed by the Secretary of State for a four-year term. Also, residents of a state bordering Illinois (Iowa, Indiana, Kentucky, Missouri, Wisconsin) who work or have a place of business in Illinois can be appointed for a one-year term. Notaries must be United States citizens (though the requirement that a notary public must be a

United States citizen is unconstitutional; see Bernal v. Fainter), or aliens lawfully admitted for permanent residence; be able to read and write the English language; be residents of (or employed within) the State of Illinois for at least 30 days; be at least 18 years old; not be convicted of a felony; and not had a notary commission revoked or suspended during the past 10 years.

An applicant for the notary public commission must also post a $5,000 bond, usually with an insurance company and pay an application fee of

$10. The application is usually accompanied with an oath of office. If the Secretary of State's office approves the application, the Secretary of State then sends the commission to the clerk of the county where the applicant resides. If the applicant records the commission with the county clerk, he or she then receives the commission. Illinois law prohibits notaries from using the literal Spanish translation in their title and requires them to use a rubber stamp seal for their notarizations. The notary public can then perform his or her duties anywhere in the state, if the notary resides (or works or does business) in the county where he or she was appointed.

KENTUCKY

A notary public in Kentucky is a public servant appointed by either the Secretary of State or the Governor to administer oaths and take proof of execution and acknowledgements of instruments. Notaries public fulfill their duties to deter fraud and ensure proper execution. There are two separate types of notaries public that are commissioned in Kentucky. They are Notary Public: State at Large and Notary Public: Special Commission. They have two distinct sets of duties and two different routes of commissioning. For both types of commissions, applicants must be eighteen years of age, of good moral character (not a convicted felon) and capable of discharging the duties imposed upon him/her by law. In addition, the application must be approved by one of the following officials in the county of application: a Circuit Judge, the Circuit Court Clerk, the county Judge/Executive, the County Clerk, a county Magistrate or member of the Kentucky General Assembly. The term of office for both types of notary public is four years.

A Notary Public: State at Large is either a resident or non-resident of Kentucky who is commissioned to perform notarial acts anywhere within the physical borders of the Commonwealth of Kentucky that may be recorded either in-state or in another state. In order to become a Notary Public: State at Large, the applicant must be a resident of the county from which he/she makes application or be principally employed in the county from which he/she makes the application. A completed application is sent to the Secretary of State's office with the required fee. Once the application is approved by the Secretary of State, the commission is sent to the county clerk in the county of application and a notice of appointment is sent to the applicant. The applicant will have thirty days to go to the county clerk's office where they will be required to 1.) Post either a surety or property bond (bonding requirements and amounts vary by county) 2.) Take the Oath/Affirmation of Office and 3.) File and record the commission with the county clerk.

A Notary Public: Special Commission is either a resident or non-resident of Kentucky who is commissioned to perform notarial acts either inside or outside the borders of the Commonwealth on documents that must be recorded in Kentucky. The main difference in the appointment process is that, unlike a Notary Public: State at Large, a Notary Public: Special Commission is not required to post bond before taking the oath/affirmation nor are they required to be a resident or employed in Kentucky. In addition, where a Notary Public: State at Large is commissioned directly by the Secretary of State, a Notary Public: Special Commission is appointed by the Governor on the recommendation of the Secretary of State. It is permitted to hold a commission as both a Notary Public: State at Large and a Notary Public: Special Commission, however separate applications and filing fees are required.

A Kentucky Notary Public is not required to use a seal or stamp and a notarization with just the signature of the notary is considered to be valid. It is, however, recommended that a seal or stamp be used as they may be required on documents recorded or used in another state. If a seal or stamp is used, it is required to have the name of the notary as listed on their commission as well as their full title of office (Notary Public: State at Large or Notary Public: Special Commission). A notary journal is also recommended but not required (except in the case of recording protests, which must be recorded in a well-bound and indexed journal).

LOUISIANA

Louisiana notaries public are commissioned by the Governor. They are the only notaries to be appointed for life. The Louisiana notary public is a civil law notary with broad powers, as authorized by law, usually reserved for the American style combination "barrister/solicitor" lawyers and other legally authorized practitioners in other states. A commissioned notary in Louisiana is a civil law notary that can perform/prepare many civil law notarial acts usually associated with attorneys and other legally authorized practitioners in other states, except represent another person or entity before a court of law for a fee (unless they are also admitted to the bar). Notaries are not allowed to give "legal" advice, but they are allowed to give "notarial" advice - i.e., explain or recommend what documents are needed or required to perform a certain act - and do all things necessary or incidental to the performance of their civil law notarial duties. They can prepare any document a civil law notary can prepare (to include inventories, appraisements, partitions, wills, protests, matrimonial contracts, conveyances, and, generally, all contracts and instruments in writing) and, if ordered or requested to by a judge, prepare certain notarial legal documents, in accordance with law, to be returned and filed with that court of law.

MAINE

Maine notaries public are appointed by the Secretary of State to serve a seven-year term. Maine is one of three states (Florida and South Carolina are the others) where a notary public can solemnize the rites of matrimony (perform a marriage ceremony). Also, licensed Maine attorneys have all of the powers of notaries public and are authorized to do all acts that may be done by notaries public.

MARYLAND

Maryland notaries public are appointed by the governor on the recommendation of the secretary of state to serve a four-year term. New applicants and commissioned notaries public must be bona fide residents of the State of Maryland or work in the state. An application must be approved by a state senator before it is submitted to the secretary of state. The official document of appointment is imprinted with the signatures of the governor and the secretary of state as well as the Great Seal of Maryland. Before exercising the duties of a notary public, an appointee must appear before the clerk of one of Maryland's 24 circuit courts to take an oath of office.

A bond is not required. A notary is required to keep a log of all notarial acts, indicating the name of the person, their address, what type of document is being notarized, the type of ID used to authenticate them (or that they are known personally) by the notary, and the person's signature. The notary's log is the only document for which a notary may write their own certificate.

MINNESOTA

Minnesota notaries public are commissioned by the Governor with the advice and consent of the Senate for a five-year term. All commissions expire on 31 January of the fifth year following the year of issue. Citizens and resident aliens over the age of 18 years apply to the Secretary of

State for appointment and reappointment. Residents of adjoining counties in adjoining states may also apply for a notary commission in Minnesota. Notaries public have the power to administer all oaths required or authorized to be administered in the state; take and certify all depositions to be used in any of the courts of the state; take and certify all acknowledgments of deeds, mortgages, liens, powers of attorney and other instruments in writing or electronic records; and receive, make out and record notarial protests. The Secretary of State's website provides more information about the duties, requirements and appointments of notaries public.

MONTANA

Montana notaries public are appointed by the Secretary of State and serve a four-year term. A Montana notary public has jurisdiction throughout the states of Montana, North Dakota, and Wyoming. These states permit notaries from neighboring states to act in the state in the same manner as one from that state under reciprocity, e.g., as long as that state grants notaries from neighboring states to act in their state. [Montana Code 1-5-605]

NEVADA

The Secretary of State is charged with the responsibility of appointing notaries by the provisions of Chapter 240 of the Nevada Revised Statutes. Nevada notaries public who are not also practicing attorneys are prohibited by law from using "notario", "notario publico" or any non-English term to describe their services. (2005 Changes to NRS 240)

Nevada notary duties: administer oaths or affirmations; take acknowledgments; use of subscribing witness; certify copies; and execute jurats or take a verification upon oath or affirmation.

The State of Nevada Notary Division Page provides more information about duties, requirements, appointments, and classes.

NEW JERSEY

Notaries are commissioned by the State Treasurer for a period of five years. Notaries must also be sworn in by the clerk of the county in which he or she resides. One can become a notary in the state of New Jersey if he or she: (1) is over the age of 18; (2) is a resident of New Jersey OR is regularly employed in New Jersey and lives in an adjoining state; (3) has never been convicted of a crime under the laws of any state or the United

States, for an offense involving dishonesty, or a crime of the first or second degree, unless the person has met the requirements of the Rehabilitated Convicted Offenders Act (NJSA 2A:168-1). Notary applications must be endorsed by a state legislator.

Notaries in the state of New Jersey serve as impartial witnesses to the signing of documents, attests to the signature on the document, and may also administer oaths and affirmations. Seals are not required; many people prefer them and as a result, most notaries have seals in addition to stamps. Notaries may administer oaths and affirmations to public officials and officers of various organizations. They may also administer oaths and affirmations in order to execute jurats for affidavits/verifications, and to swear in witnesses.

Notaries are prohibited from pre-dating actions; lending notary equipment to someone else (stamps, seals, journals, etc.); preparing legal documents or giving legal advice; appearing as a representative of another person in a legal proceeding. Notaries should also refrain from notarizing documents in which they have a personal interest.

Pursuant to state law, attorneys licensed in New Jersey may administer oaths and affirmations.

NEW YORK

New York notaries are empowered to administer oaths and affirmations (including oaths of office), to take affidavits and depositions, to receive and certify acknowledgments or proof of deeds, mortgages and powers of attorney and other instruments in writing; to demand acceptance or payment of foreign and inland bills of exchange, promissory notes and obligations in writing, and to protest these (that is, certify them) for non-acceptance or non-payment. They are not empowered to marry couples, their notarization of a will is insufficient to give the will legal force, and they are strictly forbidden to certify "true copies" of documents. Every county clerk's office in New York must have a notary public available to serve the public free of charge.

Admitted attorneys are automatically eligible to be notaries in the State of New York, but must make an application through the proper channels and pay a fee.

New York notaries initially must pass a test and then renew their status every 4 years.

OREGON

Oregon notaries public are appointed by the Governor and commissioned by the Secretary of State to serve a four-year term. Oregon notaries are empowered to administer oaths, jurats and affirmations (including oaths of office), to take affidavits and depositions, to receive and certify acknowledgments or proof of deeds, mortgages and powers of attorney and other instruments in writing; to demand acceptance or payment of foreign and inland bills of exchange, promissory notes and obligations in writing, and to protest these (that is, certify them) for non-acceptance or non-payment. They are also empowered to certify "true copies" of most documents. Every court clerk in Oregon is also empowered to act as a notary public, although they are not required to keep a journal. Oregon formerly required that impression seals be used, but now it is optional. The ink seal must be in black ink. Beginning in 2001, all Oregon notaries were required to pass an open-book examination to receive their commission. Beginning in 2006, new notary applicants were also required to complete a free three-hour online or live in-person instructional seminar, however this requirement is waived for notaries who are renewing their commissions, as long as the commission is renewed before its expiration date. Oregon law specifically prohibits the use of the term "notorio publico" by a notary in advertising his or her services, but translation of the title into other languages is not restricted.

PENNSYLVANIA

A notary in the Commonwealth of Pennsylvania is empowered to perform seven distinct official acts: take affidavits, verifications, acknowledgments and depositions, certify copies of documents, administer oaths and affirmations, and protest dishonored negotiable instruments. A notary is strictly prohibited from giving legal advice or drafting legal documents such as contracts, mortgages, leases, wills, powers of attorney, liens or bonds.

SOUTH CAROLINA

South Carolina notaries public are appointed by the Governor to serve a ten-year term. All applicants must first have that application endorsed by a state legislator before submitting their application to the Secretary of State. South Carolina is one of three states (Florida and Maine are the others) where a notary public can solemnize the rites of matrimony (perform a marriage ceremony) (2005). If you live in South Carolina but work in North Carolina, Georgia or Washington, DC, these states will permit you to become a notary public for their state. South Carolina does not offer this provision to out-of-state residents that work in South Carolina (2012).

UTAH

Utah notaries public are appointed by the Lieutenant Governor to serve a four-year term. Utah used to require that impression seals be used, but now it is optional. The seal must be in purple ink.

VIRGINIA

A Virginia notary must either be a resident of Virginia or work in Virginia, and is authorized to acknowledge signatures, take oaths, and certify copies of non-government documents which are not otherwise available, e.g. a notary cannot certify a copy of a birth or death certificate since a certified copy of the document can be obtained from the issuing agency. Changes to the law effective 1 July 2008 imposes certain new requirements; while seals are still not required, if they are used they must be photographically reproducible. Also, the notary's registration number must appear on any document notarized. Changes to the law effective 1 July 2008 will permit notarization of electronic signatures.

On July 1, 2012, Virginia became the first state to authorize a signer to be in a remote location and have a document notarized electronically by an approved Virginia electronic notary using audio-visual conference technology by passing the bills SB 827 and HB 2318.

WASHINGTON

In Washington State, any resident or resident of an adjacent state employed in Washington may apply to become a notary public. Applicants must obtain a $10,000 surety bond and present proof at a Department of Licensing. A notary public is appointed for a term of 4 years.

WYOMING

Wyoming notaries public are appointed by the Secretary of State and serve a four-year term. A Wyoming notary public has jurisdiction throughout the states of Wyoming and Montana. These states permit notaries from neighboring states to act in the state in the same manner as one from that state under reciprocity, e.g. as long as that state grants notaries from neighboring states to act in their state.

SOME CONTROVERSIES

A Maryland requirement that to obtain a commission, a notary declare his belief in God, as required by the Maryland Constitution, was found by the United States Supreme Court in Torcaso v. Watkins, 367 U.S. 488 (1961) to be unconstitutional. Historically, some states required that a notary be a citizen of the United States. However, the U.S. Supreme Court, in the case of Bernal v. Fainter 467 U.S. 216 (1984), declared that to be impermissible.

In the U.S., there are reports of notaries (or people claiming to be notaries) having taken advantage of the differing roles of notaries in common law and civil law jurisdictions to engage in the unauthorized practice of law. The victims of such scams are typically illegal immigrants from civil law countries who need assistance with, for example, their immigration papers and want to avoid hiring an attorney. Confusion often results from the mistaken premise that a notary public in the United States serves the same function as a Notario Publico in Spanish-speaking countries (which are civil law countries, see below). Prosecutions in such cases are difficult, as the victims are often deported and thus unavailable to testify.

THE MILITARY

Certain members of the United States Armed Forces are given the powers of a notary under federal law (10 U.S.C. Section 1044). Some military members have authority to certify documents or administer oaths, without being given all notarial powers. In addition to the powers granted by the federal government, some states have enacted laws granting notarial powers to commissioned officers.

ACKNOWLEDGMENTS FROM JUDI

I would like to reach out to my notary friends and colleagues across the country. This has been a difficult year and I admire each and every one of you for all you have done and how hard you have worked to continue to help people and provide notarial services to all who need them. Be well and be safe.

ACKNOWLEDGEMENTS
FROM DANIEL

This book was truly a labor of love on many levels. I was completely overwhelmed when I thought of all the people that have touched my life and were an inspiration for me to put this book together. First, let me thank my partner in life, my Hilary Jo. She has been there from day one and without her, my contributions for this book would not be possible. She has put up with my late-night and weekend work, phone calls at all times of the day and night (including on date nights), and my consistently asking her for her opinions about a topic. I would also like to thank my children Daryel, Demond, Terrance, Tanesha, Jerry, Jordan, Jamison, and Jonathan for challenging me to be a better father. They have truly stretched my thinking and kept me excited about life.

For the past 15 years, it has been a blessing to serve my community as a notary public. A very special thank you goes to some of my professional business partners and friends that helped me along the way: Elaine Wright Harris, Carol Salter, Marcy Tiberio, Valerie Barrett, Doug Diebolt, Allie Conner, Nicola Jackson, Susi Sivkov, Jamie Liggins, Steve Allison, Dean Calvert, Lori Hamm, Julia Von Bargen, Deirdre Waters, Bill Anderson, Laura J. Biewer, Christine Wissbrun, Ozie Stallworth and Cynthia Alexander. Their experiences really brought this book to life.

A very special acknowledgment is owed to the co-author of this book, Judith Lawrence. Judith was very instrumental in bringing all the concepts and ideas together to make this book great. It has been a pleasure working with Judith over these past few months to bring this project to life and without her, I don't think you would be reading this. Thank you, Judith, for your wisdom and courage.

PROFESSIONAL ACKNOWLEDGMENTS

We would both like to thank our friends and colleagues for the help they gave us:

- Craig Tew and the National Notary Association team of professionals.

- Kal Tabbara, President of the American Association of Notaries.

- Kathleen Butler, Executive Director of the American Society of Notaries.

- Lee Bialostok, Esquire, Notary Act.

- The entire Board of the Indiana Notary Association.

- Jane Willig, our superstar Editor for her dedication to MakeYourBusinessOurBusiness.

THANK YOU FOR READING OUR BOOK.

Daniel and I would love to hear from you. Email with questions and/or feedback at MakeYourBusinessOurBusiness@gmail.com.

READERS:

If you would like to purchase 100 copies of Make Your Business Our Business, we would like to say thank you with a $250.00 gift certificate. This is a one-time offer. The Gift Certificate will be awarded to the person who has a paid receipt for the 100 copies of the book. In order to claim this reward you may email MakeYourBusinessOurBusiness@gmail.com or, go to our website, MakeYourBusinessOurBusiness.com and contact us. We will respond within one business day. J&D